MATH FOR KNITTERS

KATE ATHERLEY

’/10

PUBLICATIONS

4th printing; July, 2026.

Nine Ten Publications Inc. | Vancouver | ninetenpublications.ca

Library and Archives Canada Cataloguing in Publication

Title: Math for knitters / Kate Atherley.
Names: Atherley, Kate, author
Identifiers: Canadiana (print) 20250274019 | Canadiana (ebook) 20250274025 | ISBN 9781738360741 (softcover) | ISBN 9781738360758 (EPUB)
Subjects: LCSH: Knitting—Mathematics. | LCSH: Knitwear—Pattern design. | LCSH: Knitting—Technique.
Classification: LCC TT820 .A84 2025 | DDC 746.43/2—dc23

Editor: Kim Werker

Copy editor: Michelle Woodvine

Technical editor: Joanna Fromstein

Illustrations and schematics: Alison Cooley

Cover and book design: Nine Ten Publications

Production of this book was made possible by the enthusiasm and financial support of knitters who pre-ordered the book long before it came out. Thank you for making it possible for this book to be made!

Visit ninetenpublications.ca for more books and booklets about how to make things, how things are made, and where our art and craft materials come from.

Printed in Canada on manufactured-in-Canada 100% post-consumer waste recycled paper.

For my parents, who were always worried that my math degree was never going to be actually put to good use.

CONTENTS

INTRODUCTION

Today, I am a knitting designer, teacher, and technical editor, but I didn't study these topics at school. I studied math.

After graduating with a university degree in theoretical mathematics, I worked in the software industry for a few years, before happily escaping to make a living in textile arts. And believe it or not (my dad never did!), I use my university degree more in this second career than I ever did in my first.

There's mathematics in every level of knitting. Designers use it to create designs and write up the patterns; knitters use it to follow those patterns and make those designs.

This book is aimed at knitters of all levels. My goal is to help you build the skills and confidence to successfully untangle the math behind buying yarn, choosing needles, getting gauge, reading and understanding patterns, and even tackling some of the more complex concepts involved in garment making, like sizing, alterations and adjustments.

The first half of the book covers general skills for reading patterns and working from them. I explain how to buy and substitute yarn, and how to handle various types of instructions that you may encounter. I walk you through what gauge really is, addressing how to check it, how to deal with it, and what to do when you can't match it. Lastly, I teach you how to deal with tricky instructions like "decrease evenly across," and "increase every 10th row 8 times."

The second half is specifically about garment patterns. I start with an explanation of garment size and fit information to help you: (a) determine if a garment pattern will fit you, and (b) choose the best size to make. The final section is all about how to make strategic alterations and adjustments, so your chosen garment will fit you exactly the way you want it to.

My approach to garment alterations is a little different from many other books and teachers. My goal is to make the task easier and reduce the math. Just because I love math and feel confident about it doesn't mean everyone else does or should. And even if you do love math, sometimes you just want to knit! This book doesn't just teach you how to do the calculations, it also addresses how to make good garment pattern (and size) choices up front so that fewer alterations are required and the ones you need are simpler and less risky.

And I promise you, none of the math in this book goes beyond core arithmetic skills: You don't need to know what pi is, you don't need to know about ratios and proportions, and there's absolutely no algebra or calculus. (And you don't even need to be good at mental arithmetic—I'm lousy at it; I never did manage to memorize all the multiplication tables!) Just grab a calculator or your phone's calculator app, and you're good to go.

P.S. The yarns I mention in the book are all fictional ones that I have invented for the sake of example; apply what I say to any commercial yarn.

CHAPTER 1

YARN SHOP MATH

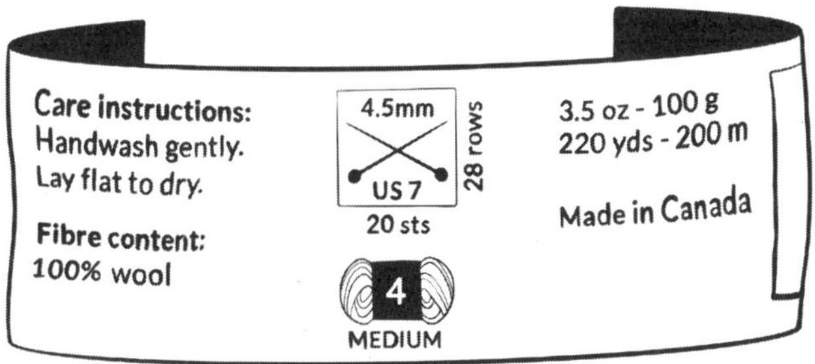

QUICK REFERENCE

- When looking at yarn specifications, only length matters. Weight (or "mass" for the scientifically inclined) does not.
- Compare units:
    - To convert yards to metres, multiply the yards by 0.91.

- To convert metres to yards, multiply the metres by 1.1.

If you have partial balls of yarn, use yarn label information and a digital scale to figure out the yardage remaining (see Calculating Yardage of Partial Balls on page 13).

MEASUREMENTS AND CONVERSIONS

1 inch = 2.54 cm

1 cm = 0.4 inch

4 inches = 10 cm

1 yard = 0.91 metre

1 metre = 1.09 yards

50 grams = 1.75 ounces

100 grams = 3.5 ounces

115 grams = 4 ounces

Note: I'm more precise when converting for length than I am when converting for weight. This is because lengths require accuracy in measuring your fabric and also for the length of yarn required. Weights are only used for designating the size of balls and skeins of yarn, and those don't need to be as precise. See sidebar, "Why Length" for more information about this.

ENOUGH YARN FOR YOUR PATTERN?

When choosing yarn for a pattern—or finding a pattern for the yarn you have—always make sure you're looking at length when you figure out how much to buy or use.

Why Length?

Some older books and patterns list yarn requirements by weight. For example, Elizabeth Zimmermann's "Pi Shawl" recipe in the Knitter's Almanac calls for "10–12 oz Shetland wool." While it may have made a bit more sense when there were fewer varieties of yarn on the market and a descriptor like "Shetland wool" was pretty unambiguous, this is not a reliable way to measure yarn.

How much a skein of yarn weighs depends on how thick the yarn is, what fibres are in it, and how it's spun. For example, 400 metres/440 yards of wool/nylon sock yarn typically weighs about 100–115 grams, or 4 ounces. But 400 metres/440 yards of a superwash worsted weight wool typically weighs about 200 grams/ 8 ounces. And there are laceweight yarns that have 400 metres/440 yards in 25 grams/1 ounce. There can also be big differences in the weight of yarns of equivalent thickness, based on the fibres: for example, cotton is a lot heavier than wool.

Calculating Yardage for Your Pattern

If the pattern lists the yarn amount in skeins or balls, multiply the number of skeins/balls by the length of yarn in each.

For example, if the pattern calls for

```
3 skeins of "Magic Merino" (225 metres per 115-gram skein)
```

This means you need

```
3 balls × 225 metres = 675 metres.
```

To figure out how much you would need of a different brand or type of yarn, divide that number by the yardage in the other brand.

For example,

```
"Woolly and Warm" comes in 50 gram (50 g) balls, which each have 140 metres.

675 metres of yarn needed ÷ 140 metres/ball = 4.82 balls.
```

If there's a fraction, always round the result of the division up. You can't buy a partial ball of yarn, of course, and you don't want to risk running short.

Note: If the fraction is really tiny (like, less than .1), then you'll probably be okay rounding down. If the result is slightly over, you can safely round down because yardage estimates listed in a pattern are just that—estimates. A responsible and sensible designer always rounds up a little, for safety's sake. More on this later, but a designer will include enough in their listed yarn requirements to provide for a swatch in a pattern, so, if you need to, you can always undo your swatch and reuse that yarn.

Watch Out: What if One Is Listed in Yards and the Other in Metres?

Some yarns are labelled in yards, some in metres. Make sure you're paying attention to the units when looking at the length of yarn, so that you're comparing like units.

Mixing Measurements: Read Carefully

Sometimes, the mass of a ball of yarn is listed in grams but the length is given in yards. It doesn't matter in the grand scheme of things, but it does mean you should always pay careful attention to the units on any measurements. If the ball size is labelled in grams, it's not safe to assume that the length will also be in given in metric units.

If the pattern lists the length of yarn in yards, and the yarn you want to buy lists it in metres, convert the pattern yardage to metres, as follows:

`Yards × .91 = metres.`

For example, if the pattern calls for 10 balls of "Super Superwash" at 220 yards per ball, that's

`10 × 220 = 2,200 yards.`

If you're buying "Fabulous & Fuzzy" to use instead, and it has 158 metres per ball, make sure you watch out for the units! First, convert one of them:

`2200 yards × 0.91 = 2,002 metres`

and

`2002 ÷ 158 = 12.6 balls of "Fabulous & Fuzzy," which you'll round up to 13.`

If the pattern lists the length in metres, but the yarn you want to buy lists it in yards, convert the pattern length to yards, as follows:

`Number of metres × 1.09 = yards.`

CALCULATING YARDAGE OF PARTIAL BALLS

Sometimes you need to figure out if a partial ball of yarn contains enough for your project. Here's how to do that.

You'll need:

- The yarn label
- A digital scale

Step 1. Weigh the partial ball.

Step 2. Divide the weight of the partial ball by the listed weight of the full skein/ball on the yarn label. For example,

`Partial ball = 42 g.`

`Full ball = 115 g.`

`42 ÷ 115 = 0.365 (which = 36.5% of a full ball).`

Step 3. Multiply that by the length of the full skein/ball, as provided on the yarn label. For example:

`Full ball = 300 yd.`

`Partial ball = 300 × 0.365 = 109.56 yd.`

Step 4. Pause and check: Does that make sense to you? The partial ball is a little more than a third of the full ball, and 109 yards is a little more than a third of 300, so that seems good!

A word to the wise: To make this easier, when I've finished a project, I like to make sure that I store any leftover partial balls of yarn with their labels.

CHAPTER 2

GAUGE MATH 101: WHAT IT MEANS, HOW TO MEASURE AND ASSESS IT, WHAT TO DO ABOUT IT

WHAT TO REMEMBER

- Stockinette stitch gauge is the most accurate way to communicate the "thickness" of yarn. But "thickness" is not a traditional or even a typical way to describe this measurement (and spinners will say that it's not even absolutely correct). The common language can get a bit confusing; for example, we often use the word "weight" when describing this measurement, but that term can get muddled up with the concept of the mass of the yarn—that is, how much it weighs on a scale.
- When buying yarn for a pattern, match the stockinette stitch gauge on the yarn label to the stockinette stitch gauge listed in the pattern.
- Checking your gauge is just about confirming that, once you've got the right type of yarn, you're using the needle size that's right for you so that the size of

your stitches leads your project to end up being the right dimensions.

QUICK REFERENCE: YARN THICKNESSES

Traditional Name	Craft Yarn Council of America (CYCA) Category	Needles Usually Recommended	Typical Gauge (Stockinette stitch over 4 inches/10 cm)
Lace	0 LACE, 1 SUPER FINE	2-4mm/US #0-6	No typical gauge
Fingering, Sock	1 SUPER FINE, 2 FINE	2-2.75mm/US #0-2	28-32 sts
Sport, Baby	3 LIGHT	3-3.5mm/US #2.5-5	24-26 sts
Double Knitting (DK), Light Worsted	3 LIGHT	3.5-4mm/US #4-6	22-24 sts
Worsted	4 MEDIUM	4.5-5mm/US #7-8	20 sts
Aran, Heavy Worsted	4 MEDIUM, 5 BULKY	4.5-5.5mm/US #7-9	18 sts
Chunky	5 BULKY, 6 SUPER BULKY	6-6.5mm/US #10-10.5	14-16 sts
Bulky	6 SUPER BULKY	8-10mm/US #11-15	12 sts
Super Bulky, Polar	7 JUMBO	12mm+/US #17+	8-10 sts

WHAT GAUGE ACTUALLY IS

Gauge is used in knitting for two reasons:

- To communicate the "thickness" of a yarn—this is the information that's listed on the yarn label, and
- A tool to make sure that your knitting will come out the right size—this is the information that's listed in your pattern.

We care about these things for a few reasons.

First, when working with a pattern, you want to choose a yarn with the appropriate thickness so that your work comes out looking the way it's supposed to look, behaving the way it's supposed to behave, and is the size you need.

And, perhaps most importantly, so that you won't run out of yarn! The yardage estimations in a pattern are dependent on you using the right yarn (and needles—more on this below).

GAUGE AS A TOOL FOR COMMUNICATING YARN "THICKNESS"

It's a straightforward concept, if a little roundabout.

It's too challenging to accurately measure the thickness of a strand of yarn, so we measure the stitches we make with that yarn instead. But stitches can be pretty small and hard to accurately measure, especially with sock or laceweight yarns, so instead of trying to measure one stitch, we measure 4 inches/10 cm of fabric and count the number of stitches (and rows) in that span of fabric.

Both yarn label and pattern have a gauge listed, so you can match them up.

Read the stockinette stitch gauge in the pattern, for example,

```
20 sts & 28 rows = 4 inches/10 cm in stockinette stitch using 4.5 mm/US #7 needles
```

and then look for a yarn that lists the same stitch and row count.

If your pattern lists gauge in a pattern stitch (e.g., garter stitch) you will need to swatch in that pattern stitch (see How to Check: A Three-Piece, One Evening Swatch, below).

Answers to Frequently Asked Questions

- Stitch gauge must absolutely match to ensure your completed project is the desired size, but there's a little bit of room for play with row gauge. If the two row gauges differ by a couple of rows, it will be fine. Find more on row gauge in this chapter's sections, Dirty Secret: Stitch Gauge is Crucial, Row Gauge Less So; and in the chapter, Gauge Math 201, Adjusting for a Different Row/Round Gauge
- If your pattern doesn't list a stockinette stitch gauge, then do an internet search on the yarn listed and use the stockinette stitch gauge the manufacturer lists. And if you can't find this information, perhaps give that pattern a miss. Yes, that's right, I'm saying that if you can't find gauge information for the yarn, skip the pattern. In this case, both the yarn and the pattern are missing key information.
- Don't worry too much about the needle size listed on the yarn label when comparing it to the needle size listed in the pattern. The needle size given is really just a suggestion, and it's not an issue if the one listed in the pattern doesn't match the needle size on the yarn label. As long as they are close—within one or two sizes—you'll be fine. If the needle size in the pattern is significantly different from the one on the yarn label, then that's a sign the yarn isn't right for that pattern. An exception is when a pattern indicates as much.
- Some patterns deliberately use a non-standard needle size to create specific effects in the fabric. This is pretty common in shawls and lace patterns: You work with a larger needle than you would to make a sweater fabric with that yarn, to create a drapey fabric.

Yarn Labels Aren't All the Same

Yarn labels don't always include every possible gauge measurement, but that doesn't mean you can't use the information they do provide.

Sometimes you only see a stitch gauge, with no row gauge. For example,

```
20 sts/4 inches.
```

This is okay; stitch gauge is generally much more important than row gauge anyway! More on this below, in the section Dirty Secret: Stitch Gauge is Crucial, Row Gauge Less So.

Sometimes a yarn label lists stitch gauge over one inch instead of four inches, for example,

```
5 sts per inch.
```

Just remember to multiply by 4!

Sometimes there's a range, for example,

```
4-6 sts per inch
```

or

```
16-20 sts/4 inches.
```

This is the yarn company acknowledging that their yarn can be used in a number of different ways.

When worked on a needle that yields a gauge matching the lower end of the range, you can assume the fabric will be looser and drapier; if working on a needle that yields a gauge matching the top of the range, the fabric will be a bit denser, a bit more structured.

Sometimes there's only a word, like "fingering" or "worsted," or a US category symbol, like the one to the right. Each corresponds to a range of expected gauges. Consult the table in the Quick Reference section at the start of this chapter to get a sense of the range, and consider whether you want a denser or looser fabric.

GAUGE AS A TOOL FOR MAKING SURE YOUR KNITTING COMES OUT THE RIGHT SIZE

When you're knitting something from a pattern, size may not matter if it's a scarf, a toy, or a baby blanket. But for garments, and accessories like hats, mittens, and socks, fit matters.

The way to make a sweater come out the right size is to make the pieces of fabric the right size. The way to make the pieces of fabric the right size is to make your stitches the right size. The designer makes all their calculations based on stitches being a specific size. To make sure that the sweater comes out right (and you don't run out of yarn), you want to check to make sure your stitches match that.

This is what we mean when we say that you should "match gauge." It means to make stitches the same size as the designer did. That's all.

Choosing the right yarn is the first step, but there is a second piece to the puzzle, which is to make sure you're using the needle size that's right for you. We all knit a little differently—some knitters pull the yarn a little tighter, some keep it a bit looser. That's fine, it's not a problem at all. But it does mean that you need to confirm the needle size that works for your own knitting style, to make your stitches the same size as the designer's.

The needle size listed in the pattern is simply the needle size the designer used when making the sample. Do you need to use the same size? Absolutely not. You just need to achieve the same stitch size, measured as gauge.

This is what swatching is all about. It's just a quick test to make sure you are using the right needles.

No one loves swatching. That's fine. You don't have to love it. No one loves waiting for the oven to preheat when you're baking cookies, but we do it because we know the end result will be better. It's a low-effort step to make sure that what you make is perfect.

And the time trade-off is so much better for knitting than for baking cookies. It takes my oven longer to preheat than it does to bake the cookies. But making a swatch is one evening, compared to the weeks it takes to finish a project. That's an investment I'm happy to make. So, if size (or yardage) matters, it's worth the time to swatch.

> ***But Will I Run Out of Yarn?***
>
> Yes, the yardage listed in your pattern absolutely includes enough to swatch. Designers are very invested in you swatching—they're expecting you to do it! So yes, there's enough yarn. And even if there isn't, swatching doesn't ruin your yarn, so, if you need to, you can undo your gauge swatch at the end of your project and reuse that yarn to finish it up.

How to Check: A Three-Piece, One Evening Swatch

Plain or Pattern: What to Swatch?

If the project you're making is worked mostly in stockinette stitch, then swatch in stockinette stitch. If your project is worked all (or mostly) in a pattern stitch—for example, garter, seed stitch, lace—and that gauge is listed, you should swatch in that pattern stitch.

Note: Any gauge listing should indicate the pattern stitch it's measuring. If there's just numbers but no pattern stitch listed, and it's a plain pattern, you can safely assume stockinette stitch. If there are multiple pattern stitches used in the project and the gauge indicator doesn't tell you what was measured, that's a pattern that is missing key information.

Testing, Testing! Three Needle Sizes

Look at the needle size listed in the pattern and grab that size, one size smaller, and one size larger.

Tip: If you know from experience that you're a looser knitter (faster knitters, or those using wooden or plastic needles often find that their stitches are a little looser), then adjust your set of three needle sizes downward, the largest should be the one listed in the pattern, and then grab the two sizes down from that. Conversely, if you're a tighter knitter (or perhaps use slippery metal needles), then use the size listed in the pattern as the smallest, and go up two sizes from there.

How Many Stitches?

Look at the gauge listed in the pattern—the number of stitches over 4 inches/10 cm. Multiply that by 1.5. That's the number of stitches you need to cast on. We knit more than 4 inches/10 cm so you have a good tidy middle section to measure. (Edges are often wonky; you don't want to try to measure them.)

What to Knit

Using the smallest of your needles, cast on. Knit 4 rows, then work in pattern until the piece is about 3 inches/8 cm tall, ending with a WS row. Knit 2 rows to make a dividing line. Change to the middle size needle and work another 3 inches/8 cm, again ending with a WS row. Knit 2 rows to make another dividing line. Change to the larger size needle and work another 3 inches/8 cm. Knit 4 rows and bind off.

Three-piece swatch.

Hold the Garter!

Many instructions for swatches have you work a few stitches at the edges in garter stitch. I don't recommend this! They can distort the fabric by compressing the edges. And contrary to popular belief, a garter stitch edge doesn't help things lie any flatter.

Make It Lie Flat

Washing (a.k.a. "blocking") the swatch is important! You need to wash the fabric before you measure it to give it a chance to relax and settle. Knit fabrics (and some yarns) often stretch out a bit with washing—it's no good to knit a sweater and then have it stretch out and become too big the first time you wash it.

Wash it the way the yarn label tells you to, and the way you intend to wash the finished item. You often see the word "block" being used. Although it's often associated with stretching an item out for drying, that's actually just one special case. Although this is a longer discussion, the short answer, really, is that to "block" your knitting simply means to wash and dry it the way you plan to take care of it.

Wash Your Woollies!

All knit pieces will need to be washed at some point. You might want to freshen them up after a few wears, or rinse out spilled coffee, and at the very least, you should always wash them once a year, before you put them away for the summer. Moths are less attracted to the wool itself, and more interested in the stuff that's on the wool: food crumbs, discarded hair and skin cells, the oils from your hair and your skin.... Putting unwashed woollies away in the spring is like putting out a sign for an all-you-can-eat moth buffet!

Measure

Use a firm ruler, not a tape measure. Count the number of stitches in 4 inches/10 cm, in the middle of each of the three sections, and count the number or rows in 2 inches/5 cm. If the yarn texture varies, measure in a few different places and take the average.

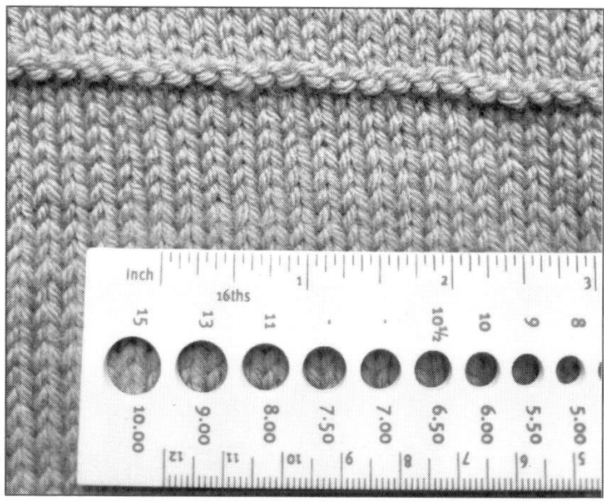

Counting the stitches in 2 inches / 5 cm.

Decide

Compare the numbers from the three sections against the gauge listed in the pattern. If you've chosen an appropriate yarn, then chances are one of the three needles you've used will get you what you need. If you hit the number exactly with one of your three needle sizes, write that down, take a moment to celebrate, and cast on!

> ***Swatching in the Round***
>
> If the pattern is worked in the round—a sock, mitten, hat—then you need to swatch in the round, too.
>
> For the average knitter a purl stitch is larger than a knit stitch. This is because, when forming a purl stitch, the yarn takes a slightly longer path around the needle, and this extra bit of yarn gets taken up into the stitch. This is normal, and nothing at all to worry about—and when you're working flat, making both knit and purl stitches, it generally all averages out and isn't noticeable.

But because stockinette worked in the round requires only knit stitches, the same knitter, using the same yarn and needles, will likely see a slightly different gauge when working flat versus working in the round. Most knitters have a slightly tighter gauge (i.e., more stitches per inch) working in the round. So if the project is worked in the round, swatch in the round.

The challenge with swatching in the round is that you have to cast on a lot of stitches to be able to measure a full 4 inches/10 cm flat—your piece would have to be at least 9 inches/23 cm in circumference. But never fear! There's a bit of a cheat—a sort of "fake" way to work in the round.

To fake it, you need to use a circular needle or a pair of longer double-pointed needles, but otherwise it's almost exactly the same as the standard swatch.

Cast on the required number of stitches (1.5 times the number of stitches listed for gauge in the pattern, as before), but instead of working back and forth in rows, work as follows:

Knit a row. Don't turn, but slide the stitches back to the other end of the needle. Carry the yarn loosely across the back—I like to wrap it around the left hand holding the needle—and knit the next row. Keep going like this, always sliding back and knitting, so you're working from the right side.

Everything else is the same as the flat swatch outlined above.

"Fake" in-the-round swatch.

What If...

...You're Really, Really Close?

If the gauge you need to achieve is between the number you get with two sizes of needles (the middle and largest, or the smallest and middle), you're good. Choose the needle that gets you closest to the gauge you need. The slightly fluid nature of a knit fabric will compensate for the tiny bit of difference between the gauge you're getting and the pattern gauge.

This is where changing needle material might also help. People routinely experience a difference in gauge when using the same size needles, but the needles themselves are different; many people knit a little tighter on slippery metal needles, and a little looser on more frictiony wood, bamboo or plastic needles.

...You Match (or Are Close) but You Don't Like the Fabric?

If you're matching the gauge, but the fabric is too stiff, or too holey and unstable, then it doesn't matter about the needle size —the yarn is not right for the project. Focus on how the yarn looks when you make stitches of the specified size. If it doesn't look good, that means that the yarn isn't a good choice. Choose a different pattern or choose a different yarn.

…None of Them Match?

This comes down to the fabric, and how far off you are. If the number you need is just a little off what you're getting with the smallest or largest needle, then try the next size (up or down) as appropriate. In this case, you will need to make another swatch, but just do one 3-inch/8 cm section on the chosen needle. (And don't skip the wash!)

Tip: Swatching is a bit like one of those silly games where you see how many college students can fit into a Volkswagen camper van. If you're supposed to be able to get 20 college students (stitches), and you're only getting 19, that means your college students (stitches) are too big, and you need some smaller ones…and to make smaller stitches you need to use a smaller needle. If you're supposed to be able to get 20 college students (stitches), and you're getting 21, that means your college students (stitches) are too small, and you need some bigger ones… and to make bigger stitches, you need to use a bigger needle.

If the fabric looks great but the stitch count is significantly off—by 2 or more stitches—then it's likely the wrong thickness of yarn. Change the yarn, or change the pattern.

A Small Difference Can Have a Big Impact

It doesn't sound like much, but 2 stitches in 4 inches/10 cm can make a huge difference to the finished result.

Say I'm trying to make a sweater that's 40 inches around, and the gauge listed is 20 stitches in 4 inches/10 cm, and the pattern tells me to cast on 200 stitches.

But the yarn I'm working with gives me a gauge of 18 stitches in 4 inches/10 cm, which works out to 4.5 stitches per inch.

Working 200 stitches at 4.5 stitches an inch results in a sweater that's over 44 inches around, which is a significantly different size than I desired.

`(200 ÷ 4.5 = 44.4 inches)`

And what if I manage to hit 22 stitches in 4 inches/10 cm, which is 5.5 stitches per inch?

200 stitches at 5.5 stitches per inch results in a sweater that's 36 inches around, which is significantly smaller than desired.

`(200 ÷ 5.5 = 36.4 inches)`

Dirty Secret: Stitch Gauge is Crucial, Row Gauge Less So

Unless a pattern specifically instructs otherwise, the priority is matching the stitch count. The row count is secondary. If your stitch count is right, and your row count is within a row or two —for example, 27 rows instead of 28—then you'll be absolutely fine!

This is because distances in knitting patterns are often measured as lengths rather than row counts; you might have to work slightly fewer or more rows to achieve the required distance, but it won't make the slightest bit of difference to the end result. If the pattern does do everything with specific row counts, then you might need to make some small adjustments.

If you're off by a lot—more than 10 percent—then you need to be careful. You can proceed, as long as the stitch gauge is okay and you like the fabric, but know that the yardage of yarn needed will be affected, and any sections of the pattern that have increases or decreases will need to be adjusted. See the chapter Gauge Math 201: Converting for a Different Gauge, and Garment Math 2: Alterations – Adjusting for a Different Row/Round Gauge on page 146 for more on adjusting for row gauge.

Row gauge can be affected by things other than thickness of the yarn. The softness of the yarn can be a factor, for example. Stitches worked in a yarn that's very soft and drapey will tend to squish down a bit more; stitches worked in a yarn that's a little crisp will tend to stand taller.

Could I Work a Different Size at Another Gauge?

Short answer: No. This might seem like a wonderful solution to not getting the called-for gauge—if your stitches are too small, you could follow the instructions for a larger size and it will magically all work out.

The widths might work, but that doesn't mean other things will. The first issue is that knit stitches aren't square, and the relationship/difference between your stitch gauge and the pattern's stitch gauge might not be the same as the difference between your row gauge and the pattern's row gauge. You could end up with something that's the right width but significantly off in length. Does this matter? Maybe. Some patterns —for a scarf or a drop shoulder sweater for example—give lengths as a distance measurement only. In this case, if you've got extra yarn, just work the lengths you want to hit, and don't worry about row counts. (This means that you might be reading the stitch counts for the size Large, but following the lengths for the Medium. This is okay, but it does add a bit of complexity to pattern reading and keeping track.)

But the more curves and shaping the garment has, and the more pieces that have to be sewn together, the riskier this gets. For example, I would never recommend this approach for a set-in sleeve sweater, since there needs to be a very precise relationship between the curves of the armhole and the sleeve cap, and scaling just doesn't work.

But Can't I Just Adjust the Pattern?

Yes! It is absolutely possible to adjust a pattern for a different gauge. But it's often more work than you might expect, and the more complex the structure, the more math is required.

Math-Free

- Any shawl that starts with a small stitch count and increases
- Toys

Easy Math

- Unshaped pieces like scarves, cowls, and blankets
- Top-down hats

Less Easy but Still Approachable

- Minimally shaped pieces where fit doesn't matter, like a tea cozy, poncho, or shrug
- Hats
- Socks and mittens that don't have any shaping, gussets or stitch patterns
- Drop shoulder garment

Getting Tricker

- Mittens with thumb gussets
- Socks with shaping
- Seamless raglan and circular yoke sweaters

As Much Work as Creating a New Design

- Gloves
- Anything worked in several pieces that have to be sewn together, especially those with shaping and curves
- Garments with shaping and a tailored construction
- Garments with set-in sleeves (seamless or seamed)

There are a couple of examples in the chapter Gauge Math 201: Converting for a Different Gauge to give you a sense of how it goes.

It's up to you if you want to do the work. For a more complex pattern, adjusting it for gauge is as much work as designing a new garment from scratch, and it can be time-consuming and risky…if you get it wrong, the shape can be off, your garment won't fit, the pieces won't go together, and you can easily run out of yarn.

I'll never say it's impossible; it's up to you to decide whether you're up for the challenge or not.

So. Should you do a gauge conversion?

- Do you know a lot about this type of thing—have you knitted a lot of these types of patterns?
- Do you enjoy the math?

- Do you enjoy spending time with a calculator, or at your computer?
- Do you enjoy experimenting?
- Do you have lots of yarn to work with? (Doing a gauge conversion means you're going to have to guess how much yarn is required.)

If you answered "yes" to all these questions, then go for it. However, if...

- You're not much of a math-lover,
- You're less familiar with this type of garment or pattern,
- You want a relaxing project that you can be confident about, without having to experiment and redo, or
- You just want to knit,

then the easier answer is to find a new pattern (or yarn).

Back in the day, if knitters couldn't make the yarn match the pattern, they would usually take the time to adjust or recalculate the pattern. My grandmother would do this all the time. But then, my grandmother knew a lot more about dressmaking and garment structure than many knitters know today; it was a standard subject at school—at least for girls—and there were fewer patterns to choose from. Today, there are so many more patterns available, and I can absolutely guarantee that no matter what you want to make, and what yarn you want to use, there is a pattern for you.

And experience level doesn't matter. I have a university degree in mathematics, I studied fashion design at college, and I spend most of my days working with a spreadsheet program, but I am more likely to choose a new pattern rather than reengineer one.

If you're looking to just knit, then another pattern is the quicker and easier answer.

CHAPTER 3
PATTERN READING MATH 1: REPEATS WITHIN ROWS, REPEATS OF ROWS

This section tackles a lot of the little number puzzles that come up when working through pattern instructions: repeats, increasing and decreasing evenly across.

REPEATING STITCHES

Different designers and publications use different punctuation conventions to indicate an instruction that is to be repeated.

Some use an asterisk (*), like this:

```
Row 1 (RS): *K3, p3; repeat from * to end.
```

Some use brackets, like this:

```
Row 1 (RS): (K3, p3) to end.
```

These instructions mean the same thing: that you are to keep repeating this 6-stitch pattern until you reach the end of the row.

No matter the punctuation, it's safe to assume that you will end the row having just worked p3 and your stitch count will divide evenly by 6.

Sometimes the repeat is only worked for part of the row, like this:

```
Row 1 (RS): K10, (p2, k2) 5 times, p2, k10.
```

Having a repeat count like this can help you keep track of what you're doing.

Sometimes, instead of a specific number of repeats, you might be told when to stop doing something. For example:

```
Row 1 (RS): *K3, p3; repeat from * to last 3
sts, k3
```

or

```
Row 1 (RS): (K3, p3) to last 3 sts, k3.
```

This means that you are to keep repeating k3, p3 across, until there's only 3 stitches left and then you knit those last 3 stitches. Instead of counting how many times you do the 6-stitch pattern, you just monitor how many stitches remain in the row. If you've got more than 3 stitches left, go back and do (k3, p3) again. If you've got only 3 stitches, then you are done with the repeat and should work the final instruction. In this case, that's k3.

You should always work the full instruction in the repeat—the full bracketed instruction. In this case, it means you end with p3 before you move onto the final three stitches.

A Multiple of Stitches Plus...

Sometimes instructions specify that a pattern stitch is worked across a multiple of a certain number of stitches, "plus" a few more. This is done when the pattern has an outside edge, or needs extra stitches to create symmetry on the two edges.

For example, "a multiple of 6 stitches, plus 3." This means that you can work the pattern stitch on any number of stitches that, if you subtract 3, divides evenly by 6. For example, this particular set of instructions would work on 9, 15, 21, 27, 33, 39 stitches, and so forth:

```
6 + 3 = 9

12 + 3 = 15

18 + 3 = 21

24 + 3 = 27
```

REPEATING ROWS

When you need to work the same few rows over and over again, to save space, patterns will tell you to repeat the rows.

Repeat Rows 1 and 2

For example:

```
Row 1 (RS): Knit.

Row 2 (WS): Purl.

Repeat the last 2 rows until piece measures 10 inches.
```

In this case, the number of times you're working the rows doesn't matter, you're just told to knit until a piece reaches a certain length.

When you're told to repeat a set of rows over and over again, you should finish at the end of the set of rows. In the example above, it means that you should stop after working a WS row.

Sometimes a pattern will tell you where you need to finish, like this:

```
Repeat the last 2 rows until piece measures 10
inches, ending with Row 1
```

or

```
Repeat the last 2 rows until piece measures 10
inches, ending with a WS row.
```

This type of instruction is helpful, because it's being specific about where you should end up. The formulation "ending with a RS row" means that the last thing you do before you stop is work a RS row (in this example, a knit row.)

Or you might see something like this, giving you a particular place to stop:

```
Repeat Rows 1-12 of Lace Pattern until piece
measures 6 inches/15 cm, ending with Row 6 of
Lace Pattern.
```

X Number of Times

Sometimes you are told how many times to repeat a pattern, and this can be worded different ways.

For example:

```
Row 1 (RS): Knit.

Row 2 (WS): Purl.

Work Rows 1 & 2, five times.
```

This means you've got to do 10 rows: [Row 1, Row 2], [Row 1, Row 2], [Row 1, Row 2], [Row 1, Row 2], [Row 1, Row 2].

Sometimes you're told to repeat a number of rows:

`Row 1 (RS): Knit.`

`Row 2 (WS): Purl.`

`Repeat Rows 1 & 2, five more times`

or

`Repeat Rows 1 & 2 another 5 times`

or

`Work Rows 1 & 2 an additional 5 times.`

In each of these three cases, you do the 2 rows 6 times in all, for a total of 12 rows. Do the 2 rows the first time through: Row 1 and Row 2. And then do that 2-row pattern 5 more times: [Row 1, Row 2], [Row 1, Row 2], [Row 1, Row 2], [Row 1, Row 2], [Row 1, Row 2].

The challenge is that not all patterns are written the same way. Sometimes you see something like this:

`Row 1 (RS): Knit.`

`Row 2 (WS): Purl.`

`Repeat Rows 1 & 2, five times.`

Without further information, this just isn't clear... Do you do them five times total, or do you do them once as presented, then 5 more times, for 6 in total?

Here's the issue: In casual English, we're pretty relaxed about how we use the word "repeat." At the gym, for example, you talk about doing "10 repeats" of something, which means that you do it ten times in total. But other usages have it the other way around, and the "repeat" doesn't include the first time. Indeed, many definitions of the word "repeat" include the crucial detail of performing the action again. If you're doing something again, this means that it happens after the first time has been completed.

Generally, the difference doesn't matter all that much in regular life (although it might lead to sorer arms after a workout!) but in a knitting pattern, especially if you're doing increases or decreases, you could get into trouble.

If you're not sure, reading ahead in the pattern can help. Sometimes, you might see a statement about the total number of rows to be worked, for example,

```
10 rows total.
```

Sometimes, including the row numbers can help, like:

```
Rows 2-12: Repeat the last 2 rows 5 times.
```

And if there's an increase or decrease that changes the stitch count, confirming the stitch count you need to reach will provide the clarity you need. For example,

```
Cast on 50 stitches.

Row 1 (RS): K2tog, k to end. 1 st decreased.

Row 2: Purl.

Repeat Rows 1 & 2, 9 times. 40 sts.
```

Since you started with 50 stitches and know you end up with 40, you know you will be decreasing a total of 10 stitches. Given the instructions provided, that means you'll work rows 1 and 2 a total of ten times: the first set and nine repeats of that set.

And if it's really not clear? Try contacting the designer for help, or look for a chat forum you can post a question to, or ask someone you know who has made that pattern before.

Or perhaps find another pattern?

EVERY *X* ROWS

A FORMULATION LIKE THIS IS PRETTY COMMON, PARTICULARLY in older patterns that were edited down to fit into the smallest possible number of pages in a book or magazine.

```
Work an Increase Row every 10th row.
```

```
Work a Decrease Row every 10th row.
```

There are two questions to answer with an instruction like this: how to do the increase or decrease row required, and when to do it.

How?

The pattern might well have the specific instructions for those rows; if it doesn't, I give details below, under the heading Increase and Decrease Rows: "Increase at Each End," "Decrease at Each End," "Increase at Start," "Increase at End".

When?

When you're told to do something "every 10th row," that means you are working a ten-row pattern, and you are to do that thing on one of the ten rows. Once in ten. In every ten rows, one of them will be the increase/decrease row, and the other nine will be worked without increasing or decreasing.

To be explicit: an instruction like this isn't specific about which row the increase or decrease is worked on; it's making a statement about how the increase/decrease rows are spaced out. The key for the knitter is to make sure that the placement is as consistent as possible, and that you end up with the right stitch count at the end.

There are two basic ways to approach this:

Stick the increase at the start of the group of ten, as follows:

```
Row 1: Increase row.

Rows 2–10: Work without increasing.
```

Or stick the increase at the end of the group of ten, as follows:

```
Rows 1–9: Work without increasing.

Row 10: Increase row.
```

Note: They're both entirely correct. Which to choose? Generally, out of habit, most people put the "special" row at (or near) the start of the repeating pattern. But it actually doesn't matter. When this formulation is used in a pattern, it's an indication that exact placement of the increase (or decrease) row doesn't matter.

To make it easier on yourself, I very strongly recommend that you set yourself up so that you're working the increase rows on the correct side: that is, if the increase row is specified as a RS row, make sure that you are on a RS row when you do it.

This means that if you find yourself facing a WS row when you're ready to do this instruction, you might need to do something like this:

```
Row 1 (WS): Work without increasing.

Row 2 (RS): Increase row.

Rows 8–10 Work without increasing.
```

And that's fine. As long as it's one in ten, you're good.

"Even" and "Straight"

Instead of saying "without increasing" or "without decreasing," patterns will often instruct you to work "even" or "straight." This just means that you maintain the stitch pattern without increasing or decreasing.

So if you're told to increase every tenth row, this means you've got a 10-row pattern: one of them should be the increase row, and the other nine should be worked even.

How Many Times?

Usually with an instruction like this, you're told how many times to do it, for example,

```
Work the Increase Row every 10th row, 6 times
```

or

```
Work the Decrease Row every 10th row, 6 times.
```

This means that you've got a 10-row pattern, and you need to do it until you've worked six total increase or decrease rows.

It doesn't necessarily mean you're doing 60 rows, though: When doing an instruction like this, you always stop counting after you've done the very last increase/decrease row.

What's important with this type of instruction is not the total number of rows, but the total number of times you do the "special" row, and what the spacing is between them.

HANG ON A MINUTE: This means that two different people knitting the same pattern might work different numbers of rows in this section? Yup, it's true!

If I do it like this:

```
[Increase row, 9 even rows] 5 times, increase row,
```

I've followed the instructions and I've worked 51 rows.

But if you do:

```
[9 even rows, increase row] 6 times,
```

you've worked 60 rows.

This is why an instruction like this is always followed by more information about where to end. You can expect to be told to end with a WS row, for example, and you'll likely see an instruction about working even until the piece is a certain length.

Read Ahead a Few Lines

I know that some people suggest you should read a pattern all the way through before you start knitting it. I don't find that particularly helpful, since a lot of stuff just doesn't make sense until you've got stitches on your needles. But it is a good idea to read ahead a few lines before you start each section, just to check for details on lengths you might need to hit, or which row you need to end a section with.

Example: Every 10th Row 6 Times, Every 8th Row 4 Times, Every 4th Row Twice

```
Work an increase row every 10th row 6 times, every 8th row 4 times, and every 4th row twice.
```

There's a lot of variation in how this can be read and worked. Keep it simple: work the increase/decrease row at the start of each section, like this:

```
(Increase row, 9 even rows) 6 times.

(Increase row, 7 even rows) 4 times.

(Increase row, 3 even rows), increase row.
```

In this case, you do need to do the full 60 rows in the first section, since you're told that you need to do 6 sets of 10-row spacing before you start the next instruction. But as before, stop counting after you've finished the very last increase (or decrease) row, and look for the next instruction.

Remember: what's most important is the total number of increase/decrease rows worked. The exact positioning of the rows and the total number of rows worked in this section is less crucial.

Example: On This and Every 10th Row 6 More Times, Every 8th Row 4 Times, Every 4th Row Twice

There's one more variation that you might see, which adds only a couple of words, but changes things a lot.

```
Work an increase row on this, and every 10th row 6 times, every 8th row 4 times, and every 4th row twice.
```

In this version you're being specifically instructed where to place the first one, which sets the placement of the rest. Also note that there's one more increase worked than in the previous example.

```
Increase row

(9 even rows, increase row) 6 times.

(7 even rows, increase row) 4 times.

(3 even rows, increase row) twice.
```

Example: An Odd Number of Rows

It's not common, but once in a while you see a pattern with an odd number of rows in the repeat. For example, you might be told to increase every 5 rows.

That is, you work an increase row and then 4 even rows. This means that you'll end up having to alternate between RS and WS increase rows, like this:

```
RS increase row, even WS row, even RS row, even WS row, even RS row.
```

```
WS increase row, even RS row, even WS row, even RS row, even WS row.
```

and so forth.

These are a little bit more challenging to keep track of than patterns with an even number of rows, and they're also a little bit more challenging to work, because you do end up having to fuss with both RS and WS increase or decrease rows.

My solution for this is to fudge the numbers a little. I'd take one out of the number of rows after the first increase, and add to the number of rows after the second.

That is, instead of doing

```
Increase row, 4 even, increase row, 4 even,
```

I would do

```
Increase row, 3 even, increase row, 5 even.
```

This way it's the same overall number of rows, and now the increases are all neatly on the RS.

When working in the round, it doesn't matter, you're always on the RS.

How to Keep Track

This is entirely up to you! Some people use row-counter apps or tools. I always keep a notebook, pen and pencil in my knitting bag, so I can do it on paper. This means that I have a record of what I've done in case I need to do it a second time, on the second sleeve or sock or mitten!

INCREASE AND DECREASE ROWS: "INCREASE AT EACH END," "DECREASE AT EACH END," "INCREASE AT START," "INCREASE AT END"

Some patterns give specific instructions for an increase or decrease row, spelling out what increase to work and where in the row to do it. For example,

```
Increase row (RS): K2, m1r, k to last 2 sts,
m1l, k2. 2 sts increased.
```

Some patterns use a more casual version, however, e.g.:

```
Increase at each end of the row.

Decrease at each end of the row.

Increase at the start of the row.

Increase at the end of the row.

Decrease at the start of the row.

Decrease at the end of the row.
```

These types of non-specific increase and decrease instructions are common, as they're a concise way of expressing a frequently used step.

For example, decreasing at each end of a row is used for armhole and sleeve cap shaping in garments; increasing at each end of a row is used for sleeve shaping and several common shawl shapes.

Whenever you encounter an instruction like this, unless otherwise instructed, always set yourself up to work the increases or decreases on a RS row. There are more options for RS increases and decreases—and they're easier to work and keep track of.

Types of Increase

There are two categories of increase: the "make 1" family and the "work twice into one stitch" family.

"Make 1" increases: these include m1r (make one right) and m1l (make one left), m1-backwards loop, a twisted yarnover, and right-leaning and left-leaning increases (RLI and LLI). In each case, the increase creates a new stitch between existing stitches.

"Work twice" increases: the most common ones are kfb—knit into front and back of the stitch—and pfb—purl into front and back of the stitch. These increases have two drawbacks: they're visible (they create a visible little bump to the left of the stitch), and they're asymmetrical. Another issue, for these purposes, is that they mess with your counting. Unless the pattern specifically uses work-twice increases, stick with increases from the "make 1" family.

A Simple "Make 1" Increase

M1L and M1R are the most common "make 1" increases, but there's another option, which I personally prefer. Make a backwards loop (also known as an "e-wrap") and just place this loop on the right-hand needle. We sometimes teach this method for casting on—it's actually not great in that situation as the resulting edge can be hard to knit from—but it does

> make a quick and easy increase. The e-wrap doesn't require you to remember the steps of make 1, and it's effectively neutral; because you don't work into this new loop until the following row—that is, you don't establish it as a knit or a purl stitch—it's well-suited for increasing in a ribbing or textured stitch pattern. I often use this one in place of both M1L and M1R in the same project, even though technically this means I'm working the same increase on both sides. I find it that it's barely noticeably, especially for things like sock toes and mitten thumbs. If you want truly "paired" increases, you can twist the loop in one direction for M1L and in the other direction for M1R.

Increase at Each End

If the Edges Are Going to Be Sewn Together, Like a Sweater Sleeve

If you're using the make 1 increases, m1r and m1l or LLI and RLI, use this version:

`RS row: K2, make-1, k to last 2 sts, make-1, k2.`

For tidiness, many knitters like to work m1r/RLI for the first one and m1l/LLI for the second one.

If you're using KFB (or PFB), use this version:

`RS row: K1, kfb, k to last 3 sts, kfb, k2.`

If the Edges Are Going to Be Visible, Like a Shaped Baby Blanket or Dishcloth

`RS row: K1, make-1, k to last st, make-1, k1.`

For tidiness, many knitters like to work m1r/RLI for the first one and m1l/LLI for the second one.

If you're using KFB (or PFB), use this version:

```
RS row: Kfb, k to last 2 sts, kfb, k1.
```

Increase at the Start

See above, but skip the second increase.

Increase at the End

See above, but skip the first increase.

Decrease at Each End

Choose the version based on how you want the edges to look.

This version aligns the lean of the decrease with the edge, for a smoother look:

```
RS row: K1, ssk, k to the last 3 sts, k2tog, k1.
```

This version aligns the lean of the decrease in opposition to the edge, for a decorative look:

```
RS row: K1, k2tog, k to the last 3 sts, ssk, k1.
```

If you will be seaming the two edges together, this placement puts the decreases right up against the seam. Some knitters prefer to work the decreases 2 stitches from the edge when they are going to be seamed – this makes the decreases a little bit more prominent. It's purely an aesthetic decision.

Decrease at the Start

See above, but skip the second decrease.

Increase at the End

See above, but skip the first decrease.

CHAPTER 4
PATTERN READING MATH 2: EVENLY ACROSS

To make instructions more concise—or maybe just to make them a little easier to write up—some pattern designers use an even more non-specific type of increase or decrease instruction: increase or decrease a certain number of stitches "evenly across" a row or a round.

For example, I knitted a sweater once that involved decreasing 40 stitches evenly across a row of 250 stitches!

There are a few different ways to approach these types of instructions. The good news is that as long as you end up with the right number of stitches at the end, and the required increases/decreases are not all bunched together, you're doing it right!

The details of the method I'm showing you here may well be different from what you've seen or used before, but I prefer doing it this way because it works for any situation—increases or decreases, working flat or in the round—so you only have to master the one solution.

In fact, this same method works for any type of alteration! Every single calculation or adjustment in this book is approached in exactly the same way: Once you've mastered the one method I explain, you can deal with any knitting math problem of that type!

For further details on the approach, see the chapter on Garment Math: The Calculations, in the section Method B: Stitch Counts for Hems and Lower Edges on page 158.

QUICK REFERENCE

- If the instructions aren't specific, there's more than one right answer, and you can choose how to execute them.
- Divide the stitches in the row or round you're working by the number of increases/decreases you need to do.
  - You're dividing the stitches up into sections, and you will work an increase or decrease in each section.
  - The result of the division tells you how many stitches there are in each section.
- If you're working in the round, place the increase/decrease at the start or end of each section.
- If you're working in rows (that is, flat), place the increase/decrease in the middle of each section.

The Write Stuff!

When I'm working on any sort of calculation or arithmetic, I always write it out in detail, the way I have in the examples. There are a few reasons for this.

- I'm not great at mental arithmetic, and writing it out lets me check I've done the calculation correctly—I'll add up the number of increases worked, and the total stitches.
- It helps me visualize how it's going to look in my knitting.
- I can keep track as I'm working the instruction.
- And if this is something I'll have to do a second time, perhaps on the other sleeve of a sweater, then I have a note of how I handled it and I can make the second one match.

INCREASE EVENLY ACROSS

Divide the total current stitch count in the row or round by the number of increases you have to work.

You're dividing the stitches into groups, and you need to increase somewhere within each group. If you're working in the round, place the increase at the start or end of each group. If you're working in rows, place the increase in the middle of each group.

If there's a remainder, distribute those extra stitches into some of the groups.

Increases Evenly Spaced Across the Next Round

Example: Increase 5 Stitches Evenly Spaced, in a Round of 60 Stitches

Divide the total stitch count by the number of increases you need to work, for example,

```
60 ÷ 5 = 12.
```

You've got 5 groups of 12 stitches. Because you're working in the round, place the increase at the start or end of the group.

If you're using a "make 1" increase,

```
Increase round: (Make-1, k12) 5 times
```

or

```
Increase round: (K12, Make-1) 5 times.
```

Use one of these versions if you're using KFB or PFB:

```
Increase round: (Kfb, k11) 5 times
```

or

```
Increase round: (K11, kfb) 5 times.
```

> **kfb and make-1: A Tale of Two Stitches**
> The number of stitches between the increases is one less for kfb than for Make-1, because the kfb increase uses up one of the existing stitches, whereas the make-1 increases are worked between existing stitches.

When There's a Remainder

The result of the division isn't always even. For example, you might be increasing 5 stitches in a round of 62.

$62 \div 5 = 12.4.$

That is,

$60 = 5 \times 12 + 2.$

Because the remainder is small, it's easiest to just stick the remainder at the end of the round. For example,

```
Increase round: (Make-1, k12) 5 times, k2.
```

You can also divide up the remainder and distribute it between repeats, making two of the increase groups larger.

```
Increase round: (Make-1, k12) 3 times, (Make-1, k13) 2 times.
```

And if you want, you can even distribute these larger increases groups more evenly, like so:

```
Increase round: (Make-1, k12), (Make-1, k13), (Make-1, k12), (Make-1, k13), (Make-1, k12).
```

All three of these variations of the instruction are correct. Remember, if the pattern needed a specific increase placement, the designer would have given a specific instruction.

Increases Evenly Spaced Across the Next Row.

The process is exactly the same as for working in the round; the only difference is that you will place the increase in the middle of each group of stitches.

Example: Increase 5 Stitches Evenly Spaced in a Row of 60 Stitches

```
60 ÷ 5 = 12.
```

You've got five groups of 12 stitches. Because you're working in rows, place the increase in the middle of those sections.

Use this if you're using any of the "Make-1" increases:

```
Increase row: (K6, Make-1, k6) 5 times.
```

Use this if you're using KFB or PFB:

```
Increase row: (K5, kfb, k6) 5 times.
```

Doing it by Hand is Better!

Although this method might feel a little clumsy at first (especially if you're used to using an online tool or calculator), doing it this way has a couple of important advantages. Remember that this one method is used for all of the calculations in this book—it can be used to handle literally any math problem or alteration! It's so powerful! Solving it by hand and then writing it out gives you a chance to check your numbers to make sure everything makes sense, and to tweak it if you'd like to fit your specific situation. If you're just following numbers a calculator has offered up, you're not necessarily going to know how—or even if—it works for your situation.

When There's a Remainder

The result of the division isn't always even. For example, you might be increasing 5 stitches in a round of 62.

`62 ÷ 5 = 12.4.`

That is,

`60 = 5 × 12 + 2.`

Because the remainder is small, it's easiest to just stick the remainder at the end of the round, for example,

`Increase row: (K6, Make-1, k6) 5 times, k2.`

You can also divide up the remainder and distribute it between repeats, making two of the increase groups larger.

`Increase row: (K6, Make-1, k6) 3 times, (K6, Make-1, k7) 2 times.`

And if you want, you can even distribute these the larger increases groups through the row, for example,

```
Increase row: (K6, Make-1, k6), (K6, Make-1, k7), (K6, Make-1, k6), (K6, Make-1, k7), (K6, Make-1, k6).
```

As before, all three of these variations of the instruction are correct. Remember, if the pattern needed a specific increase placement, the designer would have given a specific instruction.

Negotiation

I treat these calculations like a negotiation: I write things out, see how they look, and if I don't like the result, I adjust a little. You don't need to settle on the first result you hit.

In this case, because the answer is 7 with a remainder, the core repeat is (k3, Make-1, k4). But there are 6 left over. The solution? Split them across the start and the end, like this:

```
Increase row: K3, (k3, Make-1, k4) 8 times, k3.
```

Expanded out, if you prefer:

```
Increase row: K3, (k3, Make-1, k4), (k3, Make-1, k4), (k3, Make-1, k4), (k3, Make-1, k4), (k3, Make-1, k4), (k3, Make-1, k4), (k3, Make-1, k4), (k3, Make-1, k4), k3.
```

Or we could sprinkle those extra stitches through the row, making 6 of the repeats larger by one stitch, like this:

```
Increase row: (K4, Make-1, k4) 6 times, (k3, Make-1, k4) 2 times.
```

You could argue that this isn't as even as it could be, because the two smaller repeats are together at the end. So let's move one of them to the middle of the row:

```
Increase row: (K6, Make-1, k4) 3 times, (k3,
Make-1, k4), (k6, Make-1, k4) 3 times, (k3,
Make-1, k4).
```

Which can be shortened like this:

```
Increase row: [(K6, Make-1, k4) 3 times, (k3,
Make-1, k4)] 2 times.
```

The last two are exactly the same instruction; the second one is just written out more concisely. Use whichever version makes the most sense to you.

And remember: these answers are all correct! As long as you end up with the right number of stitches, and the increases aren't bunched together, you're good. Just add everything up for a quick check.

DECREASE EVENLY ACROSS

How you approach one of these instructions is exactly the same as for increases: Divide the total current stitch count in the row or round by the number of decreases you have to work. This gives you the number of stitches in each group. If you're working in the round, put the decrease at the start or end of the group. If you're working in rows, place the decrease in the middle of the group. If there's a remainder, distribute those extra stitches into some of the groups.

Note: There is a bit of a trick with decreasing, though: You have to pay attention to the stitch counts in each group. A decrease is worked on stitches in each group, so the number of stitches worked between the decreases is two less than the number of stitches in the group. See the examples below.

Decreases Evenly Spaced Across the Next Round

Example: Decrease 5 Stitches Evenly Spaced in a Round of 60 Stitches

```
60 ÷ 5 = 12.
```

Here's the tricky bit: the total number of stitches in each section includes the stitches to be decreased. And most decreases are worked on two stitches. If the answer is 12, then you work 10 stitches plain (that is, knitting them if you're working in stockinette stitch), and one decrease which accounts for 2 stitches.

When working in the round, place the decrease at the beginning (or end) of each section.

```
Decrease round: (K2tog, k10) 5 times
```

or

```
Decrease round: (K10, k2tog) 5 times.
```

Working with Remainders Example: Decrease 5 Stitches Evenly Spaced in a Round of 62 Stitches

What if the numbers don't divide nicely?

```
62 = 5 × 12 + 2.
```

When there's a small remainder, you can stick it before the first or after the last:

```
Decrease round: K2, (K2tog, k10) 5 times
```

or

```
Decrease round: K2, (K10, k2tog) 5 times
```

or

`Decrease round: (K2tog, k10) 5 times, k2`

or

`Decrease round: (K10, k2tog) 5 times, k2.`

DECREASE 8 STITCHES EVENLY SPACED ACROSS THE 62 STITCHES OF THE NEXT ROUND

If there's a bigger remainder, it's better to sprinkle those extra stitches through the round, as in the next example.

`62 ÷ 8 = 7.75.`

Which means that you've got a remainder of 6, if you divide by 8.

`62 = (8 × 7) + 6.`

I always start by writing out my first attempt:

`Decrease round: (K5, k2tog) 8 times, k6.`

This isn't great, though, because the spacing is off. You've got 5 stitches between decreases for most of the round, but, because you're working in the round, there's actually 11 between the last one in the round and the first one.

So instead, let's distribute some of those 6 extra stitches throughout the repeats:

`Decrease round: (K6, k2tog) 6 times, (k5, k2tog) 2 times.`

Or, to make it a bit more even, move one of the smaller repeats to the middle:

`Decrease round: (K6, k2tog) 3 times, (k5, k2tog), (k6, k2tog) 3 times, (k5, k2tog).`

Which you can shorten to:

`Decrease round: [(K6, k2tog) 3 times, (k5, k2tog)] twice.`

Decreases Evenly Spaced Across the Next Row

When you're working in rows, calculate how many stitches there are in each section using division, and place the decrease in the middle of each section.

<u>Example: Decrease 5 Stitches Evenly Spaced in a Row of 60 Stitches</u>

`60 ÷ 5 = 12.`

Place the decrease in the middle of each 12-stitch section, like this:

`Decrease row: (K5, k2tog, k5) 5 times.`

<u>Example: Decrease 5 Stitches Evenly Spaced in a Row of 62 Stitches</u>

What if the numbers don't divide nicely?

With a smaller remainder, just stick the extra stitches at the start and end.

`62 = (12 × 5) + 2.`

`Decrease row: K1, (k5, k2tog, k5) 5 times, k1.`

<u>Example: Decrease 8 Stitches Evenly Spaced Across the 62 Stitches of the Current Row</u>

With a larger remainder, distribute the extra stitches through the repeats.

`62 = 8 × 7 + 6.`

If I stick them at the end of the row, I get this:

`Decrease row: (K3, k2tog, k4) 8 times, k6.`

But this isn't good because you've got 3 stitches at the start of the row before the first decrease, and 10 after the last.

The better option is to take the 6 extra stitches and add one each to 6 of the repeats.

`Decrease row: (K4, k2tog, k4) 6 times, (k3, k2tog, k4) 2 times.`

Best of all: shuffle those two smaller repeats around so they're split up.

`Decrease row: [(K4, k2tog, k4) 3 times, (k3, k2tog, k4)] 2 times.`

CHECKING IN

Still with me?

Remember, instructions like this give you freedom. There isn't one right answer. Heck there isn't even one right way to figure out the answer! Do what makes sense to you.

Just remember to write it down so you can do it again, if you need to.

CHAPTER 5
PATTERN READING MATH 3: BUTTONHOLES

Cardigans often have buttons, and with buttons come buttonholes. Sometimes, a pattern tells you exactly how to place the buttonholes in your edging, but not always.

You'll need to figure out the buttonhole placement if the pattern hasn't been specific, if you've changed the number of stitches in the button band, or if you're adding buttons to a pattern that doesn't have them.

This is where you see the magic of the method from the previous section: You can use the same approach for buttonholes as you did for evenly distributing increases or decreases.

It's a little bit more involved, though, because we want to be really specific about where the buttonholes are placed.

WHAT TO REMEMBER

- Divide stitches up to determine spacing.
- Draw them out on a piece of paper to fine-tune placement.

DISTRIBUTING BUTTONHOLES

Step 1: How Many Stitches Do You Have?

How many stitches are there along the edging where the buttonholes are to be placed? If you're working a typical cardigan, this will be the number of stitches in the edging from the lower hem to the start of the neck opening.

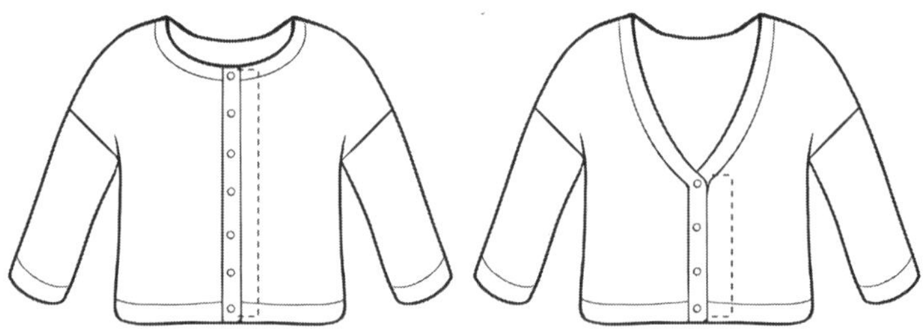

The edging of a cardigan where the buttonholes are to be placed is measured from the lower hem to the start of the neck opening.

If you're working a round neck (or any neck where the opening is perpendicular to the front opening), the front opening edgings run up all the way to cover the neck edgings.

> **To Button or Not to Button**
>
> If your garment is going to be worn open and never buttoned up, you can skip the buttonholes!

Step 2: How Many Buttonholes Do You Want?

It depends on how long the buttoned edge is, and how you want it to look.

For a standard style of closure, the lowest buttonhole should be about ¾–1 inch/2–2.5 centimetres away from the lower edge. For a round (or similar) neckline, the top buttonhole should be placed in the middle of any neckline edging.

For a V-neck, place the top buttonhole about ¾ to 1 inch/2 to 2.5 centimetres away from the start of the V-neck opening.

Then, distribute the rest of the buttons along the length of the edging, placing removable stitch markers in the fabric to mark where you want to position them. If the garment is for a body with a full bust line or if there's waist shaping, and it will be worn buttoned, place buttonholes at those points to prevent gapping. The number of buttons and the distance between them is entirely your choice, and depends somewhat on the diameter of the buttons themselves (typically, about 1–2 inches/3–5 cm for a child's garment and 2–3 inches/5–8 cm for an adult garment).

Style Rules Are Made to Be Broken!

A single button near the top of the neckline looks terrific for a swingy A-line cardigan. Or place 3 buttons around the fullest part of the bust for a feminine styling. Look at garments in your wardrobe for inspiration.

Step 3: How Big Are the Buttonholes?

That is, how many stitches do you work to create the buttonhole?

A simple eyelet buttonhole—my favourite!—uses two stitches: (yo, k2tog)

A cast on/bind off buttonhole might be worked on 4 or 5 stitches (or even more, but that's less common). Check the pattern instructions for the number of buttonhole stitches, and use those for your calculations.

Watch out! Bind-off math is tricky! Remember: Any time you bind off, you always need to add one.

For example, if you're binding off 3 stitches, you actually knit 4: knit 1, knit a second stitch, and lift the first one over (1 stitch bound off). Knit a third stitch, lift the second one over (2 stitches now bound off). Knit a fourth stitch, lift the third one over (3 stitches now bound off, 4 stitches worked).

Therefore, in the context of a buttonhole, if you are told to bind off 3, then your buttonhole is worked over 4 stitches.

Step 4: Divide and Place

Get some paper and a pencil for this. You're going to draw a picture.

> **Trust Me...It's Quicker**
>
> Yes, it's true, there are other ways of calculating this, and I know that some of them seem quicker and easier, but trust me, drawing it out helps you visualize exactly where the buttonholes are to go and gives you complete control over their placement.

Take the total number of stitches in the buttonhole band or the section of stitches where you want to place buttonholes, and divide it by the desired number of buttonholes, for example,

`100 stitches ÷ 8 buttonholes = 12.5.`

There's a remainder:

`100 = (8 × 12) + 4.`

That gives us 8 groups of 12 stitches, with 4 stitches leftover to place at the end of the row.

`(12 stitches), (12 stitches), (12 stitches), (12 stitches), (12 stitches), (12 stitches), (12 stitches), (12 stitches), 4 stitches.`

I start by placing the buttonhole in the middle of each repeat. Since I'm using (yo, k2tog), which is a 2-stitch buttonhole (BH), that gives me:

`(K5, BH, k5), (k5, BH, k5), (k5, BH, k5), (k5, BH, k5), (k5, BH, k5), (k5, BH, k5), (k5, BH, k5), (k5, BH, k5), k4.`

This puts the first buttonhole 5 stitches from the start, but the last one is 10 stitches from the end.

When making a buttonhole, we need to think about the actual position of the hole. In this case, `(yo, k2tog),` the yarnover places the actual hole to the right of the k2tog.

Which means that we have to add 1 to the number of stitches at the end of the row.

The hole is `1 + 5 + 4` stitches away from the end.

If I want to have the actual hole 5 stitches away from the end, then I've got to reduce the stitches worked at the end of the row, after the buttonhole.

Right now, the row starts and ends like this:

`K5, yo, k2tog… yo, k2tog, k5, k4.`

Put another way, like this:

`K5, yo, k2tog… yo, k2tog, k9.`

Instead of k9 at the end, I need k4, to place the hole 5 stitches from the end. I want the end of the row to go like this:

`… yo, k2tog, k4.`

Here's the original setup that I just calculated:

`(K5, BH, k5), (k5, BH, k5), (k5, BH, k5), (k5, BH, k5), (k5, BH, k5), (k5, BH, k5), (k5, BH, k5), (k5, BH, **k5**), k4.`

I need to take those extra five stitches, which I've marked out with **, and move them elsewhere in the row. Does it matter where you put them? Not really!

I'll start by adding 1 to each of the ends…

`(K5 + 1, BH, k5), (k5, BH, k5), (k5, BH, k5), (k5, BH, k5), (k5, BH, k5), (k5, BH, k5), (k5, BH, k5), (k5, BH,` ~~`k5)`~~`, k4 + 1.`

But I've still got three more to hide in the row. If I place them every other repeat or so, that is good and tidy.

`(K5 + 1, BH, k5), (k5, BH, k5 + 1), (k5, BH, k5), (k5, BH, k5 + 1), (k5, BH, k5), (k5, BH, k5 + 1), (k5, BH, k5), (k5, BH,` ~~`k5)`~~`, k4 + 1.`

Which nets out to:

`(K6, BH, k5), (k5, BH, k6), (k5, BH, k5), (k5, BH, k6), (k5, BH, k5), (k5, BH, k6), (k5, BH, k5), (k5, BH), k5.`

The spacing is slightly different between some of them, but only by one stitch. And in the grand scheme of things, that won't be visible.

CHAPTER 6
GAUGE MATH 201: CONVERTING FOR A DIFFERENT GAUGE

If your yarn doesn't match your pattern, you can choose to do a gauge conversion. (But remember that you don't have to! And often, it's a lot of complicated work. See the chapter Gauge Math 101: What It Means, How to Measure and Assess It, What to Do About It, and specifically the heading, But Can't I Just Adjust the Pattern?).

WHAT TO REMEMBER

- For any gauge conversion, you need to know the original gauge(s) the pattern was calculated for, and the gauge(s) you want to calculate for, in stockinette stitch and any relevant pattern stitches.
- Always check all dimensions of the pattern: it's not just about widths and stitches to cast on; row gauge changes can change lengths a lot, too.
- The more complex the structure, the more shaping, the more calculations you'll need to do. A spreadsheet

program—e.g., Google Sheets, Microsoft Excel, Numbers—is a fantastic tool.
- If it's a complex structure, or you don't want to do the math, a simpler solution is to find a pattern that fits your yarn.

DOING A GAUGE CONVERSION—MATH-FREE

Math-Free

- Any shawl that starts with a small stitch count and increases
- Toys

These are blissfully easy!

Using a thicker yarn and appropriate needles for that yarn will give you a larger finished piece (an even cozier shawl!). Smaller yarn and smaller needles result in a smaller piece (why is it that little stuffed toys are even cuter when they're in miniature?).

Remember, working with a different yarn will change the yardage requirements, and, unfortunately, there isn't an easy formula for this.

GAUGE CONVERSION MATH: AN OVERVIEW

There are several ways to go about doing this. The method I'm going to teach you works well for any situation, and allows you to check your work as you go.

The basic process is to determine the measurements of the

piece you're making, and calculate how to get a piece of the same measurements with a different gauge.

When considering stitch counts:

1. Get the measurement:

Divide the stitch count of the original pattern by the stitch gauge of the original yarn (stitches per inch or stitches per cm, depending on what units you're using).

2. Get the new stitch count:

Multiply that measurement by the stitch gauge of the new yarn (stitches per inch or stitches per cm, depending on what units you're using).

Then adjust the stitch count if required to fit a pattern repeat.

A lot of patterns list lengths by distance rather than row count. If you've just got a distance to work with, no calculations are required. If you're given a specific number of rows to work, this is how it goes:

1. Get the measurement:

Divide the row count of the original pattern by the row gauge of the original yarn (rows per inch or rows per cm, depending on what units you're using).

2. Get the new row count:

Multiply that measurement by the row gauge of the new yarn (rows per inch or rows per cm, depending on what units you're using).

Then adjust the row count if required to fit a pattern repeat.

There are examples below that show you how the process works.

DOING A GAUGE CONVERSION—EASY MATH

Easy Math

- Unshaped pieces—scarves, cowls, blankets
- Hats

Note: In all examples in this section, I'm including both metric and inches. Just follow the calculations for the measurement system you're most comfortable with.

Example 1: A Garter Stitch Scarf

A garter stitch scarf pattern lists gauge as 20 stitches per 4 inches/10 cm, and has you cast on 45 stitches.

What if you wanted to use a yarn that that works up at 16 stitches per 4 inches/10 cm? How many stitches should you cast on?

First you need to figure out what the width of the scarf should be based on the original gauge. Divide to determine how many stitches the original gauge is per inch/cm.

For the original yarn:

20 sts ÷ 4 inches = 5 stitches per inch.

20 sts ÷ 10 cm = 2 stitches per cm.

45 cast-on stitches ÷ 5 stitches per inch = 9 inches.

`45 cast-on stitches ÷ 2 sts per cm = 22.5 cm.`

The cast-on edge of the scarf is 9 inches/22.5 cm wide.

To figure out how many stitches to cast on with the new yarn, you need to multiply that width by the number of stitches you're getting per inch/cm with your new yarn.

Divide to determine how many stitches you're getting per inch/cm.

For the new yarn:

`16 sts ÷ 4 inches = 4 stitches per inch.`

`16 sts ÷ 10 cm = 1.6 stitches per cm.`

Then multiply the original width by that stitch count:

`9 inches × 4 stitches per inch = 36 stitches.`

`22.5 cm × 1.6 stitches per cm = 36 stitches.`

How long to knit? Typically, the pattern will tell you to work until you hit a certain length. Easy!

If there's a length to sort out, see below.

Example 2: A Ribbed Scarf.

A scarf in (k3, p3) ribbing is worked at 20 stitches per 4 inches/10 cm, and has you cast on 45 stitches.

Using the same measurements from the example above, the scarf is 9 inches/22.5 cm wide.

At 16 stitches per 4 inches/10 cm, the calculation suggests we should cast on 36 stitches. So far so good.

But! We need to check if the cast-on number works with the stitch pattern.

These are the instructions for the ribbing, to be worked on the original 45 stitches.

```
Row 1: (K3, p3) to last 3 sts, k3.
```

```
Row 2: (P3, k3) to last 3 sts, p3.
```

These instructions don't work out for 36 stitches; you don't have enough stitches to work across the row. Because 36 divides evenly by 6, you would get

```
(k3, p3), (k3, p3), (k3, p3), (k3, p3), (k3, p3), (k3, p3).
```

To be able to work this pattern stitch, you need a number of stitches that's a multiple of six, with an extra 3. Put another way, a multiple of 6 stitches plus 3.

The designer of the scarf has chosen to do it this way so that the edges of the scarf are symmetrical, so that the RS rows begin and end with a knit rib.

For this scarf pattern to work, you need to either add or subtract three, giving you a choice of 33 or 39 stitches.

Both those numbers are fine, but either way, the adjusted scarf is going to be a slightly different size from the original.

If you cast on 33 stitches, your scarf will be

33 ÷ 4 = 8.25 inches (33 ÷ 1.6 = 20.6 cm)

wide; if you cast on 39 stitches, your scarf will be

39 ÷ 4 = 9.75 inches (39 ÷ 1.6 = 24.375 cm) wide.

Does it matter? Not for a scarf! But that difference becomes a lot more important if you've got multiple pieces to sew together, or something has to fit, or there's other shaping to be accounted for.

On Lengths: Dealing with Specific Row Counts

Patterns may give you setup instructions and then specify a distance to work. For example, for most standard scarves with a simple pattern stitch like stockinette, you'll be aiming for something like 50–70 inches/125–180 cm or so.

On the other hand, if you're working a pattern stitch, the pattern might not list a length, it might list a number of rows.

For example, if you're making a cowl, you might be told to work until you've done a 16-round pattern four times, for a total of 64 rounds.

If you're working with a thicker yarn than the one specified in the pattern (a yarn for which the row/round gauge is a much smaller number), your cowl would turn out much taller; if you're working in a finer yarn (a yarn for which the row/round gauge is a much larger number), your cowl would turn out shorter. You can just wing it, of course, but if you want to be precise about it, you can figure out the lengths.

The good news is that it's done the same way as the widths! Just make sure you know your row/round gauge.

Let's say the original cowl is designed for a yarn at 28 rows/rounds per 4 inches/10 cm. Divide the round gauge first, to make sure you have it per inch/cm as required.

Note: I'm using rounds in this example, since a cowl is worked in the round.

```
28 rounds ÷ 4 = 7 rounds per inch.

28 rounds ÷ 10 = 2.8 rounds per cm.
```

If you're working in inches:

`64 rounds at 7 rounds per inch is 64 ÷ 7 = 9.14 inches.`

If you're working in metric:

`64 rounds at 2.8 rounds per cm is 64 ÷ 2.8 = 23 cm.`

To get 9 inches/23 cm in different yarns, divide to work out the number of rounds per inch/cm, and then multiply.

If your yarn works to 48 rounds per 4 inches/10 cm,

`48 rounds ÷ 4 = 12 rounds per inch.`

`48 rounds ÷ 10 = 4.8 rounds per cm.`

`9 inches × 12 rounds per inch = 108 rounds.`

If you're working in metric, it comes out to

`23 cm × 4.8 = 110 rounds.`

Yes! There's a tiny bit of difference between the imperial and the metric results for this calculation. It's because 4 inches doesn't exactly equal 10 cm. 4 inches = 10.16 cm. This sort of thing makes a difference if you're building bridges or airplanes or scientific equipment. But for the purposes of knitting, they're close enough—two rounds' difference when you're working over a hundred…really not so much to worry about!

If you're working a pattern stitch, you might need to round a bit anyway. In this case, neither 108 nor 110 divides evenly by 16. The closest multiple of 16 is 112, so that's what I'll work in this case.

How did I work that out?

`110 rounds ÷ 16 = 6.875.`

The result is pretty darn close to 7, so I just multiplied 16 × 7 to see what that gave me:

```
16 rounds × 7 repeats = 112 rounds.
```

Example 3: A Hat

The original pattern calls for a yarn gauge of 32 stitches/48 rounds over 4 inches/10 cm.

Divide by four if you want to work in inches (8 stitches/12 rounds per inch), and divide by ten if you want to work in cm (3.2 sts/4.8 rounds per cm).

Note: For gauge number, the fractions always matter! Never round these numbers. Stitch counts and row counts that result from calculations must be rounded to whole numbers, of course, but for gauge numbers, always leave the decimal points.

The instructions, in summary:

```
Cast on 160 stitches, and join in the
round.

Work (k2, p2) ribbing for 2 inches/5 cm;
then work even in stockinette stitch for
another 5 inches/12.5 cm.

Crown Decrease:
Round 1: (K8, k2tog) around. 16 sts
decreased, 144 sts rem.
Rounds 2, 4, 6, 8, 10, 12, 14, and 16:
Knit.
Round 3: (K7, k2tog) around. 128 sts.
Round 5: (K6, k2tog) around. 112 sts.
Round 7: (K5, k2tog) around. 96 sts.
Round 9: (K4, k2tog) around. 80 sts.
```

Round 11: (K3, k2tog) around. 64 sts.
Round 13: (K2, k2tog) around. 48 sts.
Round 15: (K1, k2tog) around. 32 sts.
Round 17: K2tog around. 16 sts.

Now, what if I want to use a yarn with a gauge of 12 stitches and 16 rounds per 4 inches/10 cm?

Step 1: Work Out the Gauge per Inch/Centimetre

Divide by 4 inches or 10 cm so you're working with 1 inch or 1 cm, as you prefer.

12 sts ÷ 4 inches = 3 stitches per inch.

12 sts ÷ 10 cm= 1.2 stitches per cm.

16 sts ÷ 4 inches = 4 rounds per inch.

16 sts ÷ 10 cm = 1.6 rounds per cm.

Step 2: How Big Is the Piece You Are Making?

Figure out how big around the original hat is (this is the circumference). This information might be in the pattern size notes, but if not, you'll have to work it out:

160 cast on stitches ÷ 8 stitches per inch = 20 inches around.

160 cast on stitches ÷ 3.2 stitches per cm = 50 cm around.

Step 3: Calculate Required Stitch Count at the New Gauge

To work out how many stitches you need at the new gauge: multiply the circumference of the original hat by the new gauge.

`20 inches at 3 stitches per inch = 20 × 3 = 60 stitches.`

`50 cm at 1.1 stitches per cm = 50 × 1.2 = 60 stitches.`

First thing to check: does the ribbing work out? Does 60 divide by 4, for (k2, p2) ribbing? Yes, it does! Nice and easy.

If it doesn't, round your stitch count to the nearest multiple of your pattern stitch. For more on this, see Garment Math 2: Alterations – Changing Edgings on page 114.

Step 4: Check Lengths

Then we have to check the length.

For the first part of the hat, knit to the distance specified in the pattern, so the difference in row gauge doesn't matter. You can work the ribbing for 2 inches/5 cm, and work even in stockinette for whatever distance you need, but you need to make sure that with the decreases, the hat will work out to be the right length.

There are 17 rounds in the crown decrease, as written. So how long is that?

`17 rounds at 12 rounds per inch, 17 ÷ 12 = 1.4 inches.`

`17 rounds at 4.8 rounds per cm, 17 ÷ 4.8 = 3.5 cm.`

The full hat length is just short of 8.5 inches/21 cm long (2 inches/5 cm for the ribbing, 5 inches/12.5 cm for the stockinette, and 1.4 inches/3.5 cm for the decreases).

But what about the new yarn with its different gauge?

As far as stitch counts go, you can work the decrease instructions exactly as written. The instructions depend on the number of stitches dividing by 10, which 60 does, nicely. And it's still 17 rounds.

But what about row length/height?

`17 rounds at 4 rounds per inch, 17 ÷ 4 = 4.25 inches.`

`17 rounds at 1.6 rounds per cm, 17 ÷ 4 = 10.65 cm.`

The crown decrease is a lot longer at the new gauge.

Is this a problem? Not at all! But it does change things. The point is you must check your lengths. Changing gauge is not just about changing the number of stitches you cast on. Keep reading, for a couple of suggestions for dealing with it.

Low-Fuss Solution for Fixing the Length

You can just adjust the length you work before you start the decreases.

The new crown decrease covers 4.25 inches/10.65 cm.

If you're aiming for a hat that is 8.5 inches/21 cm long, subtract to figure out how long the straight stockinette section should be:

`8.5 inches - 2 inches for the ribbing - 4.25 inches for the crown decrease = 2.25 inches`

for the straight stockinette section, instead of the 5 inches called for in the original pattern.

`21 cm - 5 cm for the ribbing - 10.65 cm for the crown decrease = 5.35 cm` for the straight stockinette section, which is much shorter than the length called for in the original pattern.

If you do this, your new hat will be a fairly different shape than the original one. The straight stockinette section is nearly 3 inches/8 cm shorter.

Does that matter? It depends on the hat, and the person wearing it.

If you were working stripes or a chart or a pattern stitch before the decreases begin, you might not have enough room to fit it all in. And it means that the hat starts getting narrow much lower down, which might not work on a head that's got a lot of hair.

More Precise Solution for Fixing the Length: Adjust the Decreases

There's another way to handle this, to recalculate the decreases so they fit into fewer rounds and take up less space.

As written, you divide the 160 stitches of the original hat up into 16 groups of 10 sts.

(That first decrease round is written to work on any multiple of 10 stitches, and the adjusted hat is 6 groups of 10 stitches.)

But if we do this a different way? 60 stitches divides neatly by 10, of course.

`60 ÷ 10 = 6.`

Instead of 6 groups of 10 stitches, what happens if we divide the stitches up into 10 groups of 6 stitches?

In that case, the decrease goes like this:

> **Round 1:** (K4, k2tog) around. 10 sts decreased, 50 sts rem.

Rounds 2, 4, 6 and 8: Knit.
Round 3: (K3, k2tog) around. 40 sts.
Round 5: (K2, k2tog) around. 30 sts.
Round 7: (K1, k2tog) around. 20 sts.
Round 9: K2tog around. 10 sts.

This is 9 rounds. If we look at the round gauge, which we calculated earlier, we can figure out how deep this is.

9 rounds ÷ 4 rounds per inch = 2.25 inches.

9 rounds ÷ 1.6 rounds per cm = 5.625 cm.

Getting better! It's definitely shorter.

If you want to match the original length, multiply the original length of the crown decrease, as we calculated from the pattern, by the new round gauge, to see what you've got to work with:

1.4 inches × 4 rounds per inch = 1.4 × 4 = 5.6 rounds.

3.5 cm × 1.6 rounds per cm = 3.5 × 1.6 = 5.6 rounds.

If we skip the even rounds, then the decrease fits neatly into 5 rounds, which is just about what we need.

Round 1: (K4, k2tog) around. 10 sts decreased, 50 sts rem.
Round 2: (K3, k2tog) around. 40 sts.
Round 3: (K2, k2tog) around. 30 sts.
Round 4: (K1, k2tog) around. 20 sts.
Round 5: K2tog around. 10 sts.

But! This looks different! Instead of 16 wedges at the top, you've now got 10.

Does that matter? It depends on the pattern. Perhaps the 16 wedges line up with a particular pattern stitch. Perhaps it's done for a decorative effect. Or perhaps it doesn't matter at all.

There's no right or wrong answer here, just options. This is the fun (and challenge) of designing: figuring out what works, and how it looks.

CHECK IN

Having fun? Do you enjoy doing these sorts of calculations?

If so, then proceed—you can do it!

But if not, that's fine, too! I absolutely 100 percent guarantee you can find a pattern that works for you that requires no math at all.

GOING FURTHER

The good news is that the calculations we did to convert scarf and the hat to a different gauge is exactly what you need to do for more complicated, more involved patterns. There's just more of them.

Tips:

- You need to know stitch and row gauge, and all the dimensions of your finished piece(s), so you can calculate widths and lengths.
- Check if all the pattern stitches fit into the adjusted stitch counts; if not, change the stitch counts or the stitch patterns.

- Check to see if the increase/decrease patterns fit into the adjusted stitch counts.
- See Garment Math: The Calculations – Distributing Shaping on page 162 for examples of how to "distribute shaping" in a garment context.

Adjusting for a Different Row/Round Gauge

As mentioned in the chapter Gauge Math 101: What It Means, How to Measure and Assess It, What to Do About It, it's not uncommon to match stitch gauge for a pattern but be off for row/round gauge.

For many projects, this can be accommodated.

When Not to Worry About Row Gauge (If Your Stitch Gauge Matches)

If:

- All distances in the pattern are given by length
- There's little to no shaping, and
- You have lots of yarn

then you can proceed with your project without any changes or calculations at all.

When to Adjust a Pattern for a Different Row Gauge

If:

- Your row/round gauge is close to the pattern the gauge was written for, for example, within about 10% of the original number
  - For example, if the pattern row gauge is 28 and you're getting 26–27 or 29–30, you'll be fine

- The project is worked in one piece, either flat or in the round
  - e.g:, hats, mittens
  - socks are a bit of a special case; you do need to understand the sock structure well, as there's a huge variety of constructions and some rely on row gauge a lot, and others don't
- It's a drop shoulder or raglan sleeve (seamed or seamless) garment, a seamless circular yoke, or a sleeveless top/vest

See Garment Math 2: Alterations – Adjusting for a Different Row/Round Gauge on page 146 for details on the method.

When Not to Adjust a Pattern for a Different Row Gauge (When Your Stitch Gauge Matches)

If:

- Your row/round gauge is not close to the gauge the pattern was written for, e.g., more than about 15% off the original number
  - For example, if the pattern row gauge is 28 and you're getting 20 or 35
- It's a set-in sleeve garment structure, with sleeves (seamed or seamless), or a circular yoke (sleeved or not)
- It's a garment constructed sideways—sleeve cuff to sleeve cuff

In any of these situations, the changes would be comprehensive, and complex. It would be better to find a pattern that suits the yarn gauge, or a yarn that suits the original pattern.

CHAPTER 7
GARMENT MATH 1: SIZE, FIT, AND EASE

When you're making a garment (or even an accessory like socks or a hat) that comes in more than one size, it can be tricky to work out what size is right for you, especially when the information provided is not always presented in the same way, or the pattern doesn't have all the information you need.

This section is all about interpreting the available information so you can choose the best option.

READING GARMENT SIZE INFORMATION

For a pattern that comes in more than one size, there are three kinds of information listed. There's a description of the person/thing the pattern is intended for, a description of the thing itself, and fit details.

"Size"

You often see the heading, "Size," or sometimes, "To Fit."

You might see generic terms describing relative size, for example,

`Small (Medium, Large)`

or

`XS (S, M, L, XL, 1X, 2X, 3X).`

Think of this as what you'd expect to see on the label when buying clothes in the store. This is telling you about the measurements of person that the item is intended to fit, hence, "To Fit."

This says nothing about the garment itself. If a hat is labeled as "Small," we don't actually know how big the hat is.

And without additional information, we don't know who it's for, either. For instance, a hat that offers Small, Medium and Large sizes: Are they intended for a range of adult heads? Are they for babies, children, and adults? Or newborns, one-year-olds, and two-year-olds?

It's like finding an old T-shirt in a vintage clothing shop and only being able to see the label… it might say "Medium," but we don't know what range that size falls in the middle of.

For children's patterns, you often see an age listed, for example,

`Newborn (6 months, 12 months).`

Or even a range,

`1-2 years (3–4 years, 5–6 years, 7–8 years).`

The latter is more helpful, giving you a good sense of who is supposed to wear the thing you'll make. But again, this still doesn't tell you how big the thing is. Sweaters for a newborn can be very different depending on whether they're supposed to be worn as a second layer over a one-piece bodysuit or worn like a jacket over a long sleeve-shirt and a pair of overalls.

Sometimes you'll see size numbers, for example,

`38 (40, 42, 44, 46, 48) inch chest.`

This is how men's suits and jackets are sold: The number describes the measurement of the person that is to wear it. How big a suit jacket actually is depends on the decade in which it was made: Compare the oversized pieces popular in the 1980s against the slim-fit looks that we see in the James Bond movies from the 1960s, for example. Jackets labelled as "Size 42" will be much bigger if they were made in the 1980s than if they were made in the 1960s.

Sometimes, you'll just see something more vague, like this:

`Sizes: 1 (2, 3, 4, 6, 7, 8).`

Although this doesn't provide a lot of information about the item, it is still helpful as a pattern-writing convenience, to help organize instructions. For example, "For sizes 1–4, start decreases when piece measures 10 inches/25 cm."

These size labels are the least important of the three types. They can be helpful, but you can cover everything you need to know with the other two types.

"Finished" or "Actual" Measurements

These measurements are describing the dimensions of the item when knitted.

If the finished measurement of a hat is listed as being 20 inches/50 cm around at the brim, that means that the hat will be 20 inches/50 cm around at the brim, when all the knitting and finishing tasks are done.

For a garment, you can usually expect to see at least a couple of measurements: the length, and the width or circumference of the body.

Body circumference: 32 (36, 40, 44, 48, 52, 56, 60) inches/ 81.5 (91.5, 101.5, 112, 122, 132, 142, 152.5) cm.

Length from shoulder: 20 (20, 20.5, 20.5, 21, 21.5, 21.5, 22) inches/ 51 (51, 52, 52, 53.5, 54.5, 54.5, 56) cm.

You may see more here, or the rest may be included in the schematic. (See below for information on schematics.)

Can't Find Measurements or a Schematic?

If there's no other information listed, either in text or schematic format, then the pattern is missing key information.

After all, choosing to knit a garment from a pattern is very different from shopping for clothes in a store. In the store, even if there's no labelling on the item, you can still try it on. You can't try on a pattern before you knit it. Detailed measurement information and a schematic are crucial.

A schematic is an essential source of information about how the garment is shaped, how it's made, and how it fits. A garment pattern that lacks a schematic just isn't giving you the detail you need to make informed choices about the size to make, about whether alterations are required and how to do them.

The Schematic

The schematic tells you two very important things: the structure and shape of the garment, and the measurements.

Structure and Shape

Schematics should tell you about:

- Sleeve/armhole structure—set-in sleeve or raglan
- Silhouette of the lower body—straight, A-line, tapered, or hourglass/X-line shaped
- Curve of the sleeve—tapered, straight or bell
- Shape of the neckline—round, V-neck, or something else

Other details may well be shown, too: if it has pockets; if it's a cardigan with asymmetrical or overlapping fronts; if there's a curved lower hem.

Measurements

The garment schematic below shows detailed measurements of the pieces as knitted. Where there's more than one size, the numbers for each size will be shown.

In this example, the pattern has nine sizes; the first number applies to the first size, the second number applies to the second size, and so on.

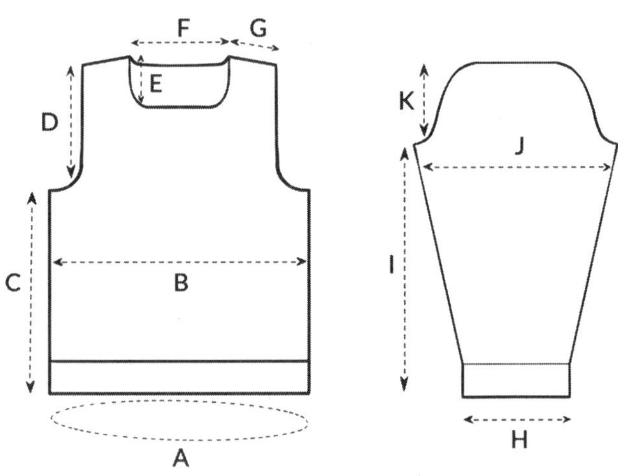

A – Body circumference: 32 [36, 40, 44, 48, 52, 56, 60, 64] inches/81 [91, 102, 112, 122, 132, 142, 152, 163] cm.

B – Body width: 16 [18, 20, 22, 24, 26, 28, 30, 32] inches/41 [46, 51, 56, 61, 66, 71, 86, 81] cm.

C – Body length to armhole: 12 inches/ 30.5 cm.

D – Armhole depth: 7.5 [7.75, 8.25, 9.25, 9.25, 9.75, 10.75, 11.25, 11.75] inches/19 [19.5, 21, 23.5, 23.5, 25, 27.5, 28.5, 30] cm.

E - Front neck depth: 3.75 [3.75, 3.75, 4.25, 4.25, 4.25, 4.75, 4.75, 4.75] inches/9.5 [9.5, 9.5, 11, 11, 11, 12, 12, 12] cm.

F - Shoulder width: 3 [3.5, 3.5, 4.25, 4.5, 4.75, 5, 5.5, 5.5] inches/7.5 [9, 9, 11, 11.5, 12, 12.5, 14, 14] cm.

G - Back width at neck: 6.5 [6.5, 7, 7.25, 7.5, 7.5, 7.75, 8.25, 8.5] inches/16.5 [16.5, 18, 18.5, 19, 19, 19.5, 21, 21.5] cm.

H - Wrist circumference: 8.25 [8.25, 8.25, 9.5, 9.5, 10.25, 10.25, 10.75, 12] inches/21 [21, 21, 24, 24, 26, 26, 27.5, 30.5] cm.

I - Sleeve length: 17 [17.5, 17.5, 18, 18, 18, 19, 19, 19] inches/43 [44.5, 44.5, 45.5, 45.5, 45.5, 48.5, 48.5, 48.5] cm.

J - Upper arm circumference: 12.5 [13.75, 15, 17.5, 18.75, 20, 21.75, 23, 25] inches/32 [35, 38, 44.5, 47.5, 51, 55, 58.5, 63.5] cm.

K - Sleeve cap height: 5 [5.5, 5.75, 7, 8.75, 9.25, 9.5, 10.5, 11] inches/12.5 [14, 14.5, 18, 22, 23.5, 24, 26.5, 28] cm.

Where a dimension has only one number listed—in this case, the body length, as shown on the left-hand side—it means that all sizes have the same measurement for that dimension.

Where there's a straight line, that's indicating that the measurement is taken from the two ends. When there's a curved line or a circle, that's indicating that the measurement relates to the full circumference.

In this example, there are arrows at the ends of the lines, to make it easy to find them; sometimes you see dots at the ends of lines. But these are just decorative elements: What's important is where the line starts and ends.

It is possible to draw a schematic for a garment pattern that doesn't have one, but it's not an easy task. Better to find a pattern that has one.

Ease or Fit Recommendation

This is how you actually choose the size. It can be phrased in a number of different ways, but the objective is the same: to give you a sense of which one you should make, based on your own body measurements.

It might be casual, like this:

```
Garment is intended to be worn oversized.
```

or

```
Choose the size closest to your own body measurements.
```

It might use some numbers, like this:

`Choose the size that's 2–3 inches larger around than your own body, measured under the arms.`

Or it might be phrased with reference to the word "ease," for example,

`Choose a size with about 4 inches of positive ease.`

Ease-y Does It

Ease describes how you're wearing a garment. Ease is the difference between your body measurement and the measurement of the garment that's on your body.

In garment patterns, ease is always relative to the measurement of the torso (the circumference of the below the underarms).

Other types of patterns should clearly tell you what measurement to consider. For example, sock fit is relative to foot circumference, and mittens relative to the circumference of your hand.

You wear different garments with different amounts of ease.

Positive Ease:

Your comfortably oversized winter coat? You're wearing it with positive ease. It's bigger than you.

Take the garment measurements, subtract off your own measurements. If the answer is a positive number, larger than zero, then you're wearing it with positive ease.

Zero Ease:

Wearing a camisole or tank top under a jacket? Wearing a fitted T-shirt under a sweater? That's likely to be pretty close to the same measurements as your own body. You're wearing that with zero ease. It's the same size as you. Take the garment measurements, subtract off your own measurements. If the answer is zero (or nearly), then you're wearing it with zero ease.

Negative Ease:

Socks, hats, leggings, tights, exercise wear, many undergarments—they stretch to fit. You're wearing them with negative ease. They're smaller than you.

Take the garment measurements, subtract off your own measurements. If the answer is a negative number, less than zero, then you're wearing it with negative ease.

What you want to find, in the garment sizing information, are details on how to choose which size is right for you, based on your body measurements. In knitting, it's rare that we make anything that matches our actual measurements. For example, hats and socks and fingerless mittens are generally worn with negative ease. That is, the hat should be smaller than you. Garments and full mittens are typically worn with positive ease (see sidebar, above).

Measure Your Clothes

It's remarkably instructive—and often surprising—to measure your own sweaters. Use that as a guide to what size sweaters you should be knitting!

But what if the pattern doesn't give you any such guidance? If you can find something in your own wardrobe that's similar in style and yarn weight, then use that as a guide. Or find another pattern.

A Garment Itself Doesn't Have Any Ease

The measurements of the garment, those listed in the pattern and shown on the schematic, are the measurements of the garment. There's no inherent ease in the garment itself.

And you can't say that ease is "included" in the garment measurements or schematic details.

Ease is a measurement of how someone is wearing something; it's a measurement of the difference between the body and the garment. To talk about ease requires both a body and a garment.

You could put the same sweater on five very different bodies: Each of them will wear it with different amounts of ease.

The listed garment measurements are just that: the measurement of the garments. Ease only comes into play when there's a body in the garment.

CHOOSING THE SIZE TO MAKE

For this, you also need to know your own measurements.

There's a lot of inconsistency in pattern language, and one of the biggest problems is in the words we use to describe the main part of the body of a garment, the bit that goes around your torso.

Choosing a size comes down to two things: Does the body you are knitting for have breasts, and was the garment pattern designed for bodies with breasts.

The Crucial Body Measurement

Use a fabric tape measure, and wear your usual undergarments —for example, a bra, tank top, T-shirt, or binder.

Hold the tape measure snugly under your arms – not at the fullest part! This is your chest/torso circumference. If your body has breasts, this is also sometimes referred to as the "high bust" or "upper bust" circumference.

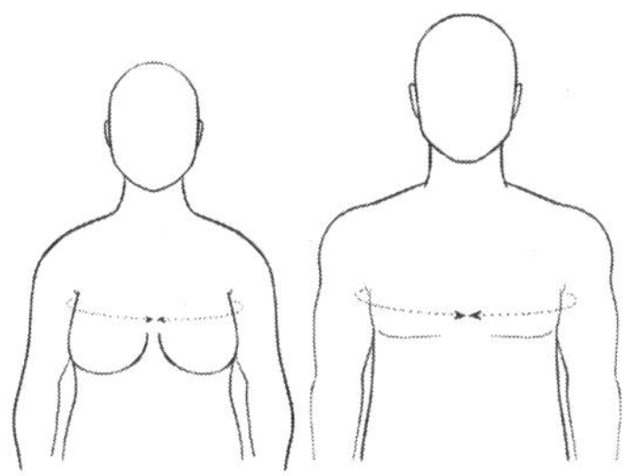

Where to measure the chest/torso circumference, also sometimes referred to as the "high bust" or "upper bust."

If your body has breasts, also take the circumference of your body around the fullest part of your bust. This is your "full bust" circumference.

Patterns for Bodies Without Breasts

Garments designed for bodies without breasts—traditionally, garments sold as being for men and children—use the word "chest."

When looking at a garment pattern, "finished chest" means the measurement of the garment body taken around the chest, under the arms.

"Chest" is also how we refer to the corresponding body measurement, the measurement you'll use to choose the size.

Taylor has a chest circumference of 34 inches/86.5 cm.

A pattern offers the following sizes:

`Finished chest: 32 (36, 40, 44, 48, 52, 56, 60) inches/ 81.5 (91.5, 101.5, 112, 122, 132, 142, 152.5) cm.`

And gives this suggestion:

`Choose a size with 2 inches/5 cm of positive ease in the chest circumference.`

Based on Taylor's body measurements, they should choose the second size, with a finished chest circumference of 36 inches/91.5 cm.

What If the Pattern Doesn't Offer a Size That Corresponds to the Pattern Recommendation?

There's a bit of wiggle room in garment sizing. You often see a range of ease, rather than just a single number. If there's a size that's close, within 1 inch/2–3 cm or so of what is recommended, go with that that size.

This ease specification is the designer's recommendation, but your own preference is important here, too. Measure something similar in your wardrobe and use that garment's measurement as a guide.

Choose another pattern. Calculating another size can be as much work as designing a new garment. It's not impossible, but it's not an easy solution, and it's beyond the scope of this book.

On Knitting Another Size at a Different Gauge

See the chapter Gauge Math 101: What It Means, How to

Measure and Assess It, What to Do About It, under the section Could I Work a Different Size at Another Gauge? on page 30.

Patterns for Bodies with Breasts

Where things get complicated is with garments designed for bodies that have breasts. Patterns that are designed for, or marketed to, women, often use "bust" to describe the measurement of the garment. For example,

`Finished Bust Circumference: 32 (36, 40, 44, 48, 52, 56, 60) inches/ 81.5 (91.5, 101.5, 112, 122, 132, 142, 152.5) cm.`

Bust is actually an odd name for this measurement. Remember, this is describing width or circumference of the garment on the body. The garment itself doesn't have breasts! The term "bust" is a rather dated convention used mostly for marketing reasons to indicate that the garment is designed for women.

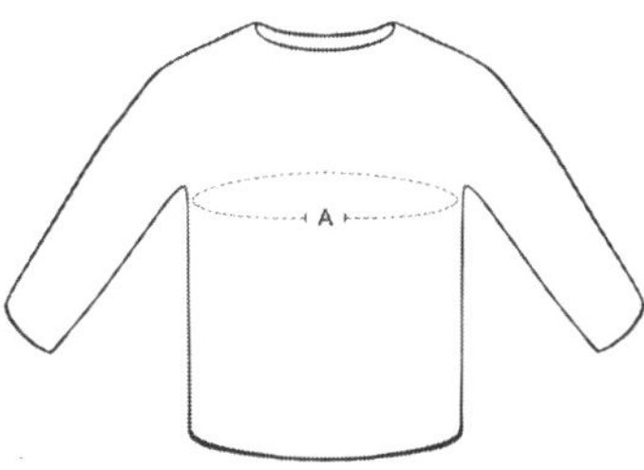

In this example, the body of the garment is unshaped, straight down from the underarm to the hem; this circumference reflects the full lower body, the full torso of the garment. In a garment that has an A-line or hourglass/X-line shape, the measurement called "bust" is always taken across or around the body under the arms (which may or may not be where your actual breasts are, of course).

When choosing a size, the word "bust" can lead us astray, especially when "Bust" gets read as "Full Bust."

For example, if a pattern tells you to choose a size with 4 inches/10 cm of positive ease in the bust circumference, you might take your own full bust circumference, add 4 inches/10 cm to that, and then choose the corresponding size.

Can you see the problem here? If you choose size based on full bust measurement, the knitter with the larger cup size is going to end up making a larger garment. And a larger garment is larger in all dimensions: sleeve circumference and length, shoulder width, neck width, neck depth, etc.

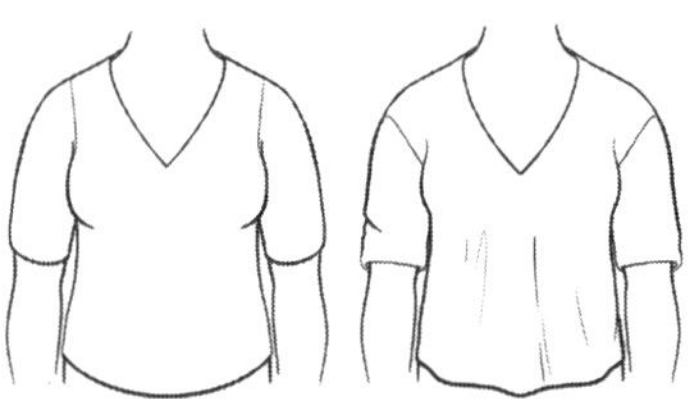

The same body size wearing a garment fitted to underarm circumference (left) vs. fitted to full bust (right).

Your full bust circumference tells me nothing about the size of your frame. It's the difference between an A cup and an F cup: Just because you have a larger cup size doesn't mean you have longer arms. Two people with wildly different full bust circumferences might have exactly the same measurements everywhere else, in which case, they should be making the same size garment.

Alternatively, you can have two people with exactly the same full bust circumference and very different frames. A taller and broader woman who wears an A cup bra could well have exactly the same size full bust circumference as a very petite woman who wears an F or G cup bra.

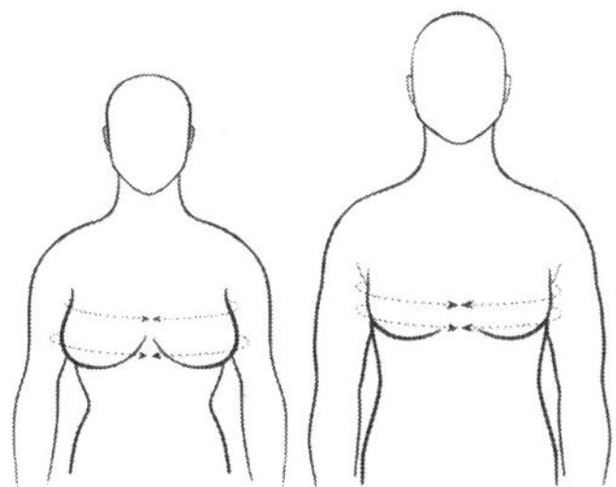

Two individuals with the same full bust circumference but different body shapes.

If the taller and broader knitter with the A cup chooses a size based on their full bust measurement, they are going to end up with a garment that is too small across the shoulders, and too short in the arms and the torso.

And women who don't have breasts don't have a "full bust" to measure.

Those who sew clothes typically work from the cross-back or cross-shoulder measurement, because these measurements better capture the overall size of the body, the frame. Unfortunately, these measurements aren't often listed in knitting patterns—at least not in a way that's easily identifiable.

The good news is that no matter how sizing is described in a pattern, the solution to choosing the right size is straightforward.

STEP 1: ALWAYS USE THE UNDERARM/UPPER BUST/HIGH BUST CIRCUMFERENCE, TO CHOOSE THE SIZE.

Consider an example:

Lee wears a bra with a D cup size. Their upper bust/torso circumference is 40 inches/102 cm, and their full bust circumference is 44 inches/112 cm.

The pattern says to choose a size with 5 inches/12.5 cm of positive ease in the body.

Lee looks at the pattern and sees that it offers the following finished sizes:

```
Finished bust: 30 (32.5, 35, 37.5, 40, 42.5, 45, 47.5, 50, 52.5, 55, 57.5, 60) inches/ 76 (82.5, 89, 95.5, 101.5, 108, 114.5, 120.5, 127, 133.5, 139.5, 146, 152.5) cm.
```

Based on the pattern recommendation, Lee would choose to make the sweater with the finished "bust" circumference of 45 inches/114.5 cm.

But there's one final check to do: Lee should make sure that the recommended size accommodates their bustline.

STEP 2: CONFIRM THAT THE CHOSEN GARMENT SIZE WILL FIT AROUND THE FULL BUST.

Hold a tape measure around your body, in a loop that matches the actual garment circumference, and move that up and down your torso. As long as the loop (the "garment") clears the full bust circumference, no accommodation is necessary.

To be explicit about this: the garment will fit more closely in the fullest part of the bust than it will in your upper torso. This is how we wear most of our clothing! Any garment that is straight—your favourite T-shirt, sweater, or blouse, sits closer to the fullest part of your bust than it does elsewhere on your body. Measuring your own clothes will confirm this. As we've already learned, too much positive ease around the fullest part of the bust can give you a garment that's too big in the shoulders. But even if the garment fits well in the shoulders, you don't want too much positive ease around the bust because this can create the effect of a "pouch" at the centre front. Look at your sewn garments made from woven fabrics—the ones with bust darts—to see how this works.

Many (store bought) garments that are made from very fine knits are designed to be worn with zero or even a very small amount of negative ease in the full bust—to skim, rather than droop.

It really is very instructive to measure your own clothes!

If the Garment Doesn't Clear the Full Bust?
Work the same pattern with one of these modifications:

- If it's only a little bit too small (e.g., less than 2 inches/5 cm), deepen the V-neck so it starts below the underarms; this adds extra space without further adjustments.
- Change the shape of the garment below the underarms; make it an A-line.
- Go with the next larger size. But be careful! The larger size will be larger in the shoulders and upper body; make sure it's not too big in those areas.
- Work the larger size for the front only. See the chapter Garment Math 2: Alterations – Different Size Front & Back on page 152.
- Change patterns:
    - Choose a style that gives room for your bustline: a deeper V-neck, or an open-front cardigan.
    - Choose a style that offers bust shaping, like darts or short rows.

Note: If the difference between your upper bust/chest

circumference and your full bust is significant, for example, if you wear a bra with a D cup or larger, and you're aiming for a more fitted garment, then I recommend choosing a pattern with darts or short rows. Yes, you could add them to a pattern that doesn't offer them, but these types of alterations are more complex, and are beyond the scope of this book. I recommend Amy Herzog's book *Knit to Flatter* for help with this (see Further Reading on page 180).

Choosing a Size: It's All Relative

Choosing the size relative to the underarm/upper bust will give you the right fit in the shoulders and neck, but what about the lower body? How do you create the shape you want?

The fit and shape of the garment below the underarms is entirely separate from the fit and shaping of the upper body—the yoke.

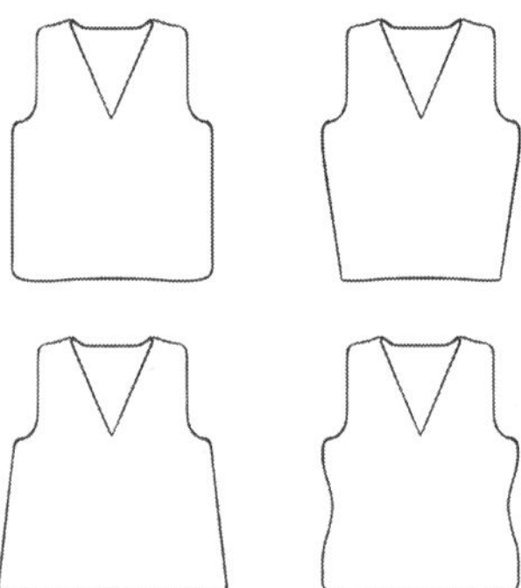

Happily, you can easily make a straight garment into another shape, like an hourglass/X-line or A-line. Similarly, you can make an hourglass/X-line shaped garment into an A-line, or straight, and you can make A-line garment straight or hourglass or tapered.

All it takes is a tape measure and a little math!

And all of this is outlined in the chapter Garment Math 2: Alterations.

A Special Case: Outliers for the Armhole Depth and Chest Circumference Relationship

Garments are designed to fit standard body measurements and proportions. That is, the designer uses a set of body measurements as guidelines to fit, and these body measurements (necessarily) make assumptions about proportions and relationships between key measurements. The obvious one is height: For example, if the body measures 60 inches/152 cm around under the arms, you will assume that this is the body of an adult rather than a child, and you will set other dimensions, like height and arm length and armhole depth to align with those assumptions.

Some bodies—most commonly those of non-average height—don't align to those average proportions. Many things, like body length, body shaping, and sleeve length, can be fixed with garment alterations below the underarm. These adjustments are covered in the chapter Garment Math 2: Alterations. The one adjustment that is more challenging is when the armhole depth for a given chest circumference isn't appropriate. A much shorter adult might need a shorter armhole depth; a much taller adult needs more depth in the garment armhole.

If this is true for the body you're knitting for, I recommend the following considerations:

- A drop shoulder garment naturally has a deeper armhole.
- It's relatively straightforward to alter the

yoke/armhole depth of a raglan (seamed or seamless), and many circular yoke designs.

- Set-in sleeves:
    - If the garment is sleeveless, the alteration is simple: Just add or remove depth in the straight section of the armhole.
    - If the garment has sleeves, the alteration is complex, requiring adjustment to the body pieces and the sleeve cap. In this case, you might find it easier to choose the garment size based on armhole depth. If you do wish to tackle this kind of alteration, I recommend Amy Herzog's *Ultimate Sweater Book* (see Further Reading on page 180).

CHAPTER 8
GARMENT MATH 2: ALTERATIONS

Not all garment alterations are the same: Some of them are significantly easier than others.

Choosing garment patterns is a bit like looking for a new home: It's easier to repaint and put up bookshelves than it is to install a whole new bathroom! Look for patterns that don't require you to make the more difficult alterations, and then customize the things that are easier to modify.

Once you've identified a garment pattern that works well for you, you can use it over and over again. Makers do this all the time: Sewists do it with clothing patterns, just as cooks and bakers do it with recipes.

In this chapter, I take you through the types of alterations you can do, and how to do them.

BE STRATEGIC ABOUT YOUR GARMENT PATTERNS

Choose a garment that offers

- The right overall size (see the chapter Garment Math 1: Size, Fit, and Ease)
- The right gauge
- The right overall structure and construction—e.g., raglan, set-in sleeve, circular yoke

... and tweak the simpler details

- Body length
- Sleeve length
- Body shape
- Edgings

...to make it perfect.

And these alterations are not just easy—they're powerful! You can radically change the look of a garment by making changes to the sleeves and body.

In this section, I'll cover these easy alterations, and a couple of common fit tweaks that use the same skills, specifically:

- Changing edgings
- Changing body length
- Changing body shape—e.g., add or remove or adjust waist shaping, add or remove A-line shaping
- Adjusting sleeve for length for longer or shorter arms
- Changing sleeve style length—e.g., wrist length vs. three-quarter vs. elbow vs. short
- Adjusting for V-necks and crewnecks: changing style and/or depth
- Working a different size front and back to accommodate a larger bust

If you want to dig deeper into garment structure and learn about how garments are designed and calculated or tackle upper body adjustments, I highly recommend The Ultimate Sweater Book, by Amy Herzog.

An Important Note About Gauge

For all the alterations covered in this section, I assume that you are working to the stitch gauge for the pattern. As discussed in the chapter Gauge Math 201: Converting for a Different Gauge, recalculating an entire garment for a different stitch gauge is a larger and complex task. But all the calculations below allow you to work to your own row/round gauge—because it's rare that you can match both. In Gauge Math 201: Converting for a Different Gauge – Adjusting for a Different Row/Round Gauge on page 84, I specifically address adjusting to accommodate a different row gauge.

Garment Alterations Degree of Difficulty Index

Math-free (or almost entirely!)

- Changing colours, adding stripes
- Changing edgings

A little math

- Changing body length
- Changing sleeve length
- Adding/removing shaping in lower body, e.g., waist shaping
- Changing neckline depth/style for crew and V-necks
- Altering yoke depth for a raglan or circular yoke

<u>More challenging</u>

- Other neckline changes
- Adding bust darts
- Adding a pattern stitch without a gauge change

<u>Essentially designing a new garment</u>

- Creating a new size
- Adjusting stitch gauge
- Adding a pattern stitch with a gauge change
- Altering yoke size or patterning for a raglan or circular yoke
- Changing armhole depth

<u>Even designers find this challenging</u>

- Changing yoke, armhole, sleeve cap construction to another structure

HOW THIS SECTION WORKS

For each alteration, I explain what you can change, and how to change it. I list what information is required, the decisions to make, and the calculations required. Since the calculation methods are the same across all types of adjustments, I've gathered the details of the methods together with some examples in the next chapter.

Once you understand the big picture, the rest is just simple arithmetic.

Complexity Rating

For each type of alteration, I've included an indicator of its complexity. If you're just starting out, read through a couple of the Level 1 (◆) and 2 (◆◆) examples. In most cases, the types of calculations you have to do for the higher-level examples are not more complicated, there are simply more of them.

In fact, even the more complex alterations, the ones beyond the scope of this book, use these same calculation methods. The reason they're more difficult is because they affect more than one aspect of the garment, and require consideration of how the garment structure works, how the elements fit together, and how they relate to the body. For example, altering the depth of the armhole on a set-in sleeve sweater is, itself, a straightforward task, but it requires also adjusting the sleeve cap so that the pieces fit together; and altering the sleeve cap requires reshaping the curve so that when it's sewn in, at an angle, it still fits. Not impossible, but requiring a lot more knowledge and calculations to make it work.

SETTING YOURSELF UP FOR SUCCESS

- Make sure the garment pattern you're working with has a schematic—a detailed diagram with measurements. (See Garment Math 1: Size, Fit, and Ease – The Schematic on page 90.)

- The key assumption here is that the garment's upper body structure and size are correct. When altering a garment, leave the upper body/yoke/sleeve cap construction alone, and maintain the stitch counts and shaping in the upper body between the neckline/

shoulders and the start of the underarm shaping. To be specific:

- If working bottom up, make any adjustments you want in the lower body and sleeves below the underarms. The key is to match the stitch counts from the pattern, just before the armhole shaping, on both sleeve and body.
- If working top down, work from the pattern until you're past the armhole shaping/separation, then do what you want.

- All of these examples assume that you are matching the stitch gauge for the pattern as written, but we will work to your own working row/round gauge.
    - Always wash the swatch (or the piece you're working on) before you measure your gauge.

- The notes below refer to "edging" and "main" fabrics. Most garment patterns are worked in more than one stitch pattern: the main section of the body in one stitch pattern or fabric, and the edges in another. For example, a lot of sweaters are worked in overall stockinette stitch, with ribbing or garter stitch used for hems, necklines, and sleeve cuffs. I'm using "edging" to refer to the stitch pattern used for those elements, and "main" fabric for the pattern stitch(es) used for the other parts of the garment.

Where Was That Again?

For information about gauge adjustments, see the chapter Gauge Math 201: Converting for a Different Gauge. For information about choosing the right size to make, see the chapter Garment Math 1: Size, Fit, and Ease.

CHANGING EDGINGS

Level of Difficulty: ◆

Changing the edgings can be remarkably transformative, completely changing the look of a garment.

Pattern Stitch

To swap out the pattern stitch, look at the stitch counts where the edgings are worked: body hems, sleeve cuffs, necklines, cardigan front openings.

In each case, confirm that your stitch pattern fits into the stitch counts, and adjust if required. For example, if you want to work (k1, p1) ribbing around a neckline or on the cuff of a sleeve worked in the round, you will need to have an even number of stitches.

Guidelines for Fitting Stitch Patterns into Hems and Edgings

- When adjusting to a specific multiple for knit/purl combination stitch patterns like ribbing and seed stitch, you'll be looking for the nearest multiple of your pattern repeat. In some cases, it might be larger than the stitch count for your main fabric. In this case, remove one repeat to round down—it's better to work the edging on a smaller stitch count than the main section, since these types of stitch patterns can be prone to stretching out.
- If you're working in the round, you need an even multiple of the pattern repeat, e.g., a multiple of 4 for (k2, p2) ribbing.
- If you're working flat, and the piece is going to be seamed on both sides, remember that the first and last

stitch of the row will disappear into the seam. Make sure your stitch count is an even multiple of your pattern repeat, plus 2. To make it easy to seam, knit the first and last stitch of the row, on all rows, and work the pattern stitch between these two edging stitches.

  - For tidiness, consider aligning the stitches on either side of the seam that so they'll fit together in pattern. That is, if you're working a back and a front in (k2, p2) ribbing, have the hem edging on the front pieces begin and end with k2 (plus seam stitch), and have the hem edging on the back pieces begin and end with p2 (plus seam stitch), so that when sewn together, you have (k2, p2) ribbing uninterrupted all the way around.

- If working a cardigan body in one piece, or the front edgings of a cardigan, you want to arrange the stitches so that they are symmetrical, beginning and ending with the same stitches. For example, if working a ribbing pattern, it looks tidiest if you begin and end the RS rows with a knit rib. For (k1, p1) ribbing, work on an odd number of stitches so the RS rows begin and end with k1. For (k2, p2) ribbing, work on a multiple of 4 stitches plus 2, so the RS rows begin and end with k2.
- If working separate cardigan fronts that will be seamed on one side, and have an edging picked up and knit on the other, see the previous example.
- If working separate cardigan fronts that will be seamed on one side, and will not have an edging picked up on the other, the stitch count matters less, but it looks tidy if you place a knit rib at the opening edge (that is, the right-hand edge of the right front, and the left-hand edge of the left front), and work the

stitch at the other edge in garter stitch, to help with seaming.

Smaller Stitch Counts, Smaller Needles

It's also a good idea to use a smaller needle than you would use for the main fabric of the garment when working a knit/purl texture pattern on an edging, especially if the body of the garment is worked in stockinette, reverse stockinette or garter stitch. For most knitters, and most knitting methods, the purl stitch is slightly larger than the knit stitch, as the yarn travels slightly further around the needle. And when transitioning between knits and purls, there's a little bit of extra yarn introduced in the spaces between the stitches, too. This means that a row that has both knit and purl stitches will use more yarn, and will be slightly wider than a row that is worked only in one stitch; an all-knit row will be the "smallest" and use the least yarn, and an all-purl row will be slightly "bigger." The more knit/purl transitions, the wider the row will get, and the more yarn used. A ribbing fabric seems to contract, in that it folds in on itself, but worked on the same size needles, ribbing will actually relax out to be wider than the same stitch count worked in stockinette stitch.

Stitch Count Transitions

If you have adjusted the stitch count for the edging pattern, you will need to work an edging/main fabric transition.

- For a top-down garment: Work the transition in the last RS row of your main pattern stitch, to the adjusted number. Then work the edging on that count.
- For a bottom-up garment: Cast on the adjusted number, and work the edging on that. Then work a transition in the first RS row of your main pattern stitch.

If the difference is only a few stitches, 2 or 3, work them close to the edges, and perhaps one in the centre; if there's more, see the chapter Pattern Reading Math 2: Evenly Across.

Depth

Edging depth is straightforward to adjust, too, and a change there can radically affect the look of a garment.

For Sleeve Cuffs and Garment Body Hems

The only consideration is whether you want to retain the same overall length. For example, if you want to make the ribbing of a sleeve cuff longer, but keep the sleeve the same length overall, from underarm to lower edge, you'll need to remove length from the main section of the sleeve. See the section on Changing Sleeve Length, on page 136, for how to handle that.

Neckline Edging Depth Changes

For a crew neck, or cardigan edgings, depth adjustments are more about style than fit: A deeper edging makes for a great fold-over collar, or a turtleneck. For a cardigan, consider whether you want the front edgings to overlap for buttoning, just meet, or not meet at all.

There is one caveat: For a V-neck pullover, increasing the edging depth can make the neck too small to put on. (This is because V-neck edgings have decreases in them, and therefore the bound-off edge gets smaller and smaller the more you work.) If you want a deeper edging for a V-neck, you're best to lower the point of the V to compensate. See Neckline Depth Adjustments later in this chapter.

CHANGING BODY LENGTH

When assessing body length measurements, always work from the full body length. That is, always work from the measurement taken from the shoulder, not from the underarm.

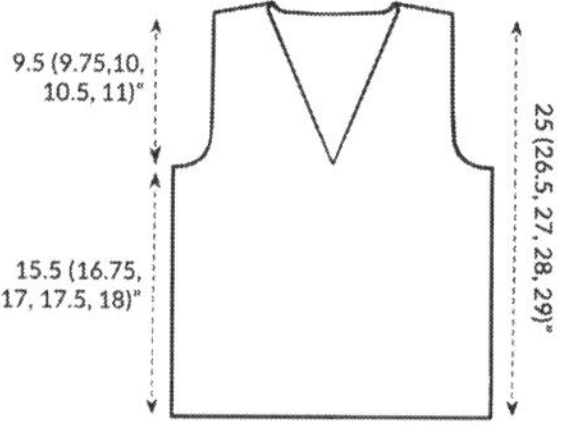

Schematic of the body of a sweater, indicating length measurements.

You can't just use the lower left measurement as an indicator of the full length, as you don't necessarily know where the armhole sits relative to your body. (It's rare that the armhole of a sweater is right up close to your actual underarm—that would make it uncomfortably tight.)

If the garment schematic lists a measurement down from the shoulder—in this example, that's the number on the right-hand side—use that. If it doesn't list the full measurement, add together the armhole depth and the lower body length.

Unshaped Body

Level of Difficulty: ◆

If the garment body is straight, this is just a case of knitting more (or less) distance, as you wish!

For example, if you determine that you need to add 2 inches, then you'll add 2 inches to the distance you work between the top of the lower edging and underarm.

Find these numbers in the pattern:

- Depth of edging (this can be customized, too)

Measure:

- Desired length between underarm and lower edge, taking into account the underarm position, as noted above

Determine (for a top-down garment only):

- Length to edging, calculated as
  - Length to edging = desired length between underarm and lower edge - edging length as written.

Working the adjusted body:

- For a bottom-up garment
  1. Cast on and work edging as written in the pattern.
  2. Work until piece measures desired length to underarm.
  3. Resume working from the pattern, beginning with armhole shaping.

- For a top-down garment
  1. Once you have completed the yoke/armhole shaping, work the desired length from underarm to edging.

2. Work the edging and bind off as written in the pattern.

Body with Hourglass/X-line Shaping

In the case of a garment with shaping, there are three different solutions, depending on what you're trying to do.

- If you want to keep the shape but adjust the body length for a taller or shorter body, see Adjust the Curves.
- If you want to extend the lower portion of the body but retain the position of any waist shaping, see Lowering the Hem.
- If you want to cut off the bottom, as if hemming a pair of pants, see Raising the Hem.
- If you want to change the circumferences as well as the lengths, see the section Adjusting Shaping on a Garment That Already Has Shaping on page 130.

Adjusting the Curves

Level of Difficulty: ◆◆

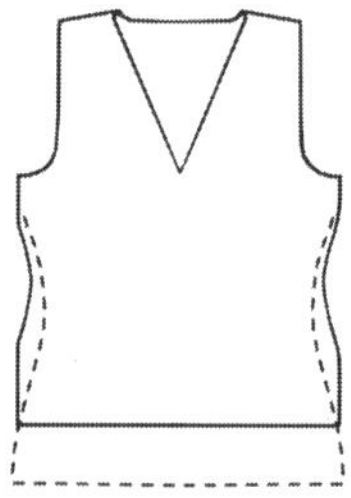

I often do this type of adjustment: making the body proportionally shorter, to accommodate my less-than-average height.

This means that I keep all the stitch counts, but adjust the lengths.

In my case, I need fewer rows/rounds between lower edge and waist, and again between waist and armhole. If you're taller, you probably need extra rows/rounds in both areas. If you're long-waisted, you might need to keep the lower edge at the same place but lower the narrowest part of the waist. That is, add more distance between waist and underarm, and reduce the distance between the waist and the lower edge.

Find these numbers in the pattern:

- Stitch count at hem, in main fabric just above the edging
- Stitch count at waist
- Stitch count just below underarms (before armhole shaping if you're working bottom up, after armhole increases if you're working top down)
- Depth of edging (this can be customized, too)

Make a note of:

- Your row/round gauge

Measure:

- Desired length between underarm and lower edge, taking into account the underarm position, as noted above
- Desired length between the lower edge and waist

Determine:

- The working lengths, calculated as

  - Lower body working length = desired length from top of lower edging to waist shaping - depth of the edging.
  - Waist to underarm working length = actual target garment length from waist to underarm.

Calculate:

- The placement of the shaping along working length between top of lower edging and waist
- The placement of the shaping along working length between waist and underarm

Both of these use the Garment Math: The Calculations – Distributing Shaping, on page 162.

Working the adjusted body:

- For a bottom-up garment
  1. Cast on and work edging as written in the pattern.
  2. Work the calculated decreases between top of lower edging and waist.
  3. Work calculated increases between waist and underarm.
  4. Resume working from the pattern, beginning with armhole shaping.

- For a top-down garment
  1. Once you have completed the yoke/armhole shaping, work the calculated shaping between underarm and waist.
  2. Work calculated shaping between waist and top of lower edging.

3. Work the edging and bind off as written in the pattern.

Lowering the Hem

Level of Difficulty: ◆

This adjustment is for when you just want to keep the body shape and shaping, but add an extension to the lower edge. For example, this is the method you use to make a hip-length sweater into a tunic.

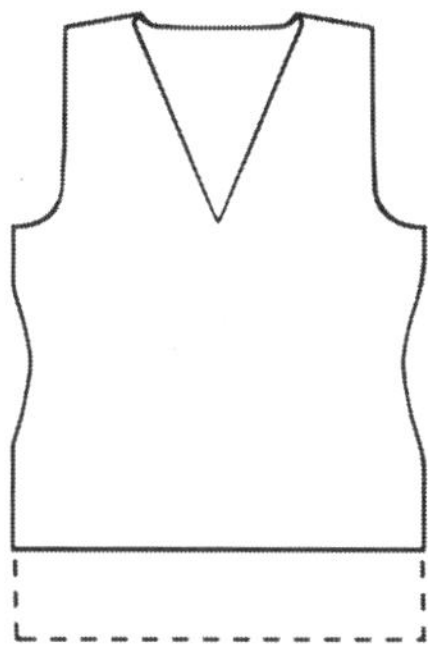

Measure:

- How much length you want to add. See the start of this section for how to measure for that.

Working the adjusted body:

- For a bottom-up garment
  1. Cast on and work edging as written in the pattern.
  2. Add the required extra length in the distance between edging and start of waist decreases.

3. Resume working from the pattern, beginning with waist shaping.

- For a top-down garment
  1. Once you reach the full stitch count for the lower body (the hip circumference), add the length you need in the main section before you start the edging.
  2. Work the edging and bind off as written in the pattern

Raising the Hem

Level of Difficulty: ◆◆◆

This adjustment is for when you just want to keep the basic shape, but change where the lower edge falls, like hemming a pair of pants.

Determine how long you want the body to be, from the underarm.

This adjustment can be simpler or more complicated, depending on what you're trying to do. When I'm shortening a garment in this way, I tend to let the pattern itself guide me.

The simplest answer is to have the garment's lower edge align with the waist. If you're working bottom up, cast on the stitch count at the waist, from the pattern, and work as written up to the underarm; if you're working top down, follow the instructions as written to the waist and stop there. The schematic should tell you how far down from the underarm the narrowest part of the waist hits, so you can get a sense of whether that suits your needs. This method will result in a garment that's a little longer than your waist because the edging is added below the narrowest part of the waist. If you want a different length or shape, refer to Adding Waist Shaping with or Without Length Adjustment to an Unshaped Garment on page 126, and Other Body Shape Changes on page 133.

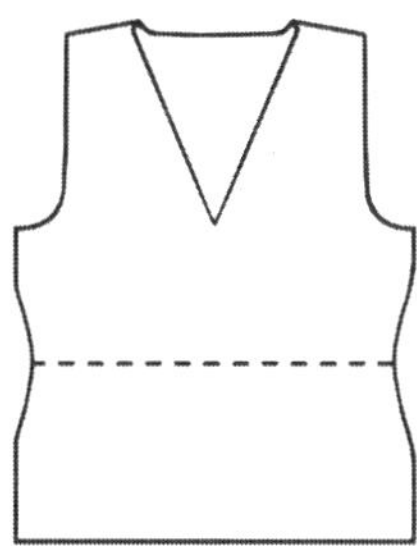

Find these numbers in the pattern:

- Stitch count at narrowest part of waist
- Stitch count for lower edging
- Stitch count at hem, in main fabric just above the edging
- Length between waist and underarm

Calculate:

Edging numbers (use Garment Math: The Calculations – Method B: Stitch Counts for Hems and Lower Edges on page 158.)

- Edging stitch count
    - Edging/Main Fabric Transition

Working the adjusted body:

- For a bottom-up garment

1. Cast on the calculated stitch count for the edging, and work the edging stitch pattern as given.
2. Work an edging/main fabric transition if required.
3. Work a short distance at the stitch count for the waist.
4. Resume working from the pattern, beginning with shaping above the waist.

- For a top-down garment
  1. Follow the pattern until you hit the stitch count and length for the waist.
  2. Work a short distance at that stitch count.
  3. Work an edging/main fabric transition if required.
  4. Work edging stitch pattern on your calculated stitch count, and bind off.

ADDING WAIST SHAPING WITH OR WITHOUT LENGTH ADJUSTMENT TO AN UNSHAPED GARMENT

Level of Difficulty: ◆◆

Use this method if you want to keep the lower stitch count the same but add waist shaping, with or without an adjustment in length. If you also want to change the lower measurements/stitch counts, see Other Body Shape Changes on page 133.

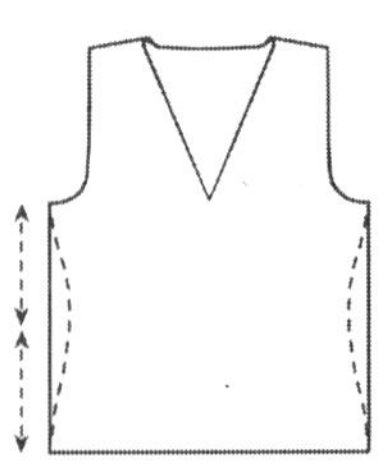

Find these numbers in the pattern:

- Stitch count just below underarms (before armhole shaping if you're working bottom up, after armhole increases if you're working top down)
- Stitch count at hem, in main fabric just above the edging
- Depth of edging (this can be customized, too)

Make a note of:

- Your stitch gauge (the assumption is that your working stitch gauge matches the gauge the pattern is calculated for. See An Important Note About Gauge in this chapter on page 110.)
- Your row/round gauge

Measure:

- Desired total length between underarm and lower edge, taking into account the underarm position, as noted above
- Desired length between waist and underarm shaping, taking into account the underarm position, as noted above
- Desired length between lower edge and waist
- The circumference of your body at the waist

Determine:

- The working lengths:
    - Lower body working length = length from lower edge to waist shaping - depth of the edging.

    - Waist to underarm working length = actual target garment length from waist to underarm.
- Desired circumferences at waist, if you are adding waist shaping. This will be your actual body measurements plus your desired ease.
    - Keep the waist ease in line with the ease for the upper bust and hips. That is, if the garment is 5 cm/2 inches larger than your body in the upper body, make the garment 5 cm/2 inches larger than your body at the waist.
    - More precisely:
        - Garment waist circumference = your actual waist circumference × Ease Factor.
    - See the "Ease Factor" sidebar for more information.

Calculate:

- Stitch count for waist (use Garment Math: The Calculations – Method A: Stitch Counts for the Middle of a Piece on page 157)
- The distribution of the shaping along working length between top of lower edging and waist
- The distribution of the shaping along working length between waist and underarm. For the latter two, use Garment Math: The Calculations – Distributing Shaping on page 162.

Working the adjusted body:

- For a bottom-up garment
    1. Cast on and work the edging stitch pattern as written.

2. Work the calculated decreases between top of lower edging and waist.
3. Work the calculated increases between waist and underarm.
4. Resume working from the pattern, beginning with armhole shaping.

- For a top-down garment
  1. Once you have completed the yoke/armhole shaping, work the calculated shaping between underarm and waist.
  2. Work the calculated shaping between the waist and the top of the lower edging.
  3. Work the edging and bind off as written in the pattern.

The Ease Factor: Determining the Circumference of Your Garment at The Waist

There should always be a little positive ease around the waist of your garment. Generally, I keep the ease at the waist in line with the fit of the garment around the chest/upper bust.

Take the circumference of your body at the underarms, and look at the circumference of the garment for your size at that point.

```
Ease factor = garment circumference at
underarms ÷ your body circumference at
underarms.
```

For example, if the original garment is 44 inches/112 cm around at the underarms, and your body is 40 inches/102 cm at that point, the Ease Factor is

```
44 inches ÷ 40 inches = 1.1.
```

Or, if you're working in metric:

```
112 cm ÷ 102 cm = 1.1.
```

To calculate the circumference of the garment at the waist, take your own waist measurement, and multiply that by the ease factor.

If your waist is 37 inches/94 cm around at the waist, to calculate the garment waist circumference, multiply that by 1.1.

```
Garment waist circumference = 37 inches
× 1.1 = 40.75 inches.
```

Or, if you're working in metric:

```
Garment waist circumference = 94 cm ×
1.1 = 103.5 cm.
```

ADJUSTING SHAPING ON A GARMENT THAT ALREADY HAS SHAPING

If you're working from a pattern that already has waist/lower body shaping, and you want to adjust the shape of the garment, there are different solutions, depending on what you're looking to achieve.

- If you wish to retain all measurements/stitch counts, and only change lengths, see this chapter, Changing Body Length – Body with Hourglass/X-line Shaping on page 120.

- If you wish to adjust the waist shaping, but leave the other stitch counts (widths/circumferences) alone, see this chapter, Adding Waist Shaping with or Without Length Adjustment to an Unshaped Garment on page 126.
- If you wish to adjust the lower edge measurement, but leave the waist and other body stitch counts (widths/circumferences) alone, see immediately below.
- If you to adjust more than one aspect, whether lengths or widths/circumferences, see this chapter, Other Body Shape Changes on page 133.

Adjusting the Lower Edge of an Hourglass/X-line Shaped Garment with or Without Length Adjustment

Level of Difficulty: ◆◆

Find these numbers in the pattern:

- Stitch count at existing waist
- Stitch counts at existing hem (in main fabric just above the edging and in the edging pattern)
- Depth of edging (this can be customized, too)

Make a note of:

- Your stitch gauge (the assumption is that your working stitch gauge matches the gauge the pattern is calculated for. See this chapter, An Important Note About Gauge on page 110.)
- Your row/round gauge

Measure:

- Desired length between lower edge and waist
- The circumference of your body where you want the lower edge to hit

Determine:

- The working length
    - Lower body working length = desired length from lower edge to waist shaping - depth of the edging.
- Desired garment circumference at lower edge. This is your actual body measurement plus your desired ease.

Calculate:

- Stitch counts for lower section. Use Garment Math: The Calculations – Method B: Stitch Counts for Hems and Lower Edges on page 158.
    - Edging stitch count
    - Stitch count in main fabric (above the edging)
    - Edging/main fabric transition
- Then:
    - Distribute shaping along working length between top of lower edging and waist

Working the adjusted body:

- For a bottom-up garment
    1. Cast on calculated the stitch count for the edging and work the edging stitch pattern as given.
    2. Work an edging/main fabric transition if required.
    3. Work the calculated shaping between top of lower edging and waist.
    4. Resume working from the pattern, beginning with the waist.

- For a top-down garment
    1. Work from pattern until you have completed the waist shaping.
    2. Work the calculated shaping between waist and top of lower edging.
    3. Work an edging/main fabric transition if required.
    4. Work edging stitch pattern on your calculated stitch count, and bind off.

OTHER BODY SHAPE CHANGES

Level of Difficulty: ◆◆◆

This method allows you to create any size, length or shape you want in the lower body: A-line, tapered, or hourglass/X-line.

Instead of altering what's already written, we start from scratch, giving you full flexibility. The only thing that's fixed in this case is the stitch count below the underarms, the rest is your choice!

Find these numbers in the pattern:

- Stitch count just below underarms (before armhole shaping if you're working bottom up, after armhole increases if you're working top down)
- Stitch counts at existing hem (in main fabric just above the edging and in the edging pattern)
- Depth of edging (this can be customized, too)

Make a note of:

- Your stitch gauge (the assumption is that your working stitch gauge matches the gauge the pattern is calculated for. See this chapter, An Important Note About Gauge, on page 110)
- Your row/round gauge

Measure:

- Desired total length between underarm and lower edge, taking into account the underarm position, as noted above
- If you want waist shaping: desired lengths between lower edge and waist, and between waist and underarm shaping
- The circumference of your body at the key points (where you want the lower edge to hit, and at waist if you want shaping at that point)

Determine:

- The working lengths
  - If making a tapered or A-line garment,

        - `Working body length = length from lower edge to the underarm - the depth of the edging.`
    - If making an hourglass/X-line garment
        - `Lower body working length = length from lower edge to waist shaping - depth of the edging.`
        - `Waist to underarm working length = actual target garment length from waist to underarm.`
- Desired garment circumference at key points (lower edge, and waist if desired). These will be your actual body measurements + your desired ease.
    - If adding waist shaping to a garment that doesn't have it, keep the waist ease in line with the ease for the rest of the garment body. See this chapter, Adjusting the Lower Edge of an Hourglass/X-line Shaped Garment with or Without Length Adjustment, on page 131, for more on this..

Calculate:

- Stitch counts for lower edge (use Garment Math: The Calculations – Method B: Stitch Counts for Hems and Lower Edges on page 158)
    - Edging stitch count
    - Stitch count in main fabric (above the edging)
    - Edging/main fabric transition
- Stitch count for waist, if required (use Garment Math: The Calculations – Method A: Stitch Counts for the Middle of a Piece on page 157)
- If making a tapered or A-line garment
    - Distribute shaping along working length between top of lower edging and underarm (see Garment

Math: The Calculations – Distributing Shaping on page 162)

- If making an hourglass/X-line garment
  - Distribute shaping along working length between top of lower edging and waist, and also along working length between waist and underarm (see Garment Math: The Calculations – Distributing Shaping on page 162)

Working the adjusted body:

- For a bottom-up garment

1. Cast on calculated the stitch count for the edging, and work the edging stitch pattern as given.
2. Work an edging/main fabric transition if required.
3. Work the calculated shapings between top of lower edging and underarm.
4. Resume working from the pattern, beginning with armhole shaping.

- For a top-down garment

1. Once you have completed the yoke/armhole shaping, work the calculated shaping between underarm and top of edging.
2. Work an edging/main fabric transition if required.
3. Work edging stitch pattern on your calculated stitch count, and bind off.

CHANGING SLEEVE LENGTH

To alter the sleeve length, you need to know the structure of the sleeve/body join, and where the underarm of the sleeve hits your body.

Set-in sleeves and raglans worked in pieces have sleeve caps. Drop shoulder garments do not; the sleeve is straight across the top.

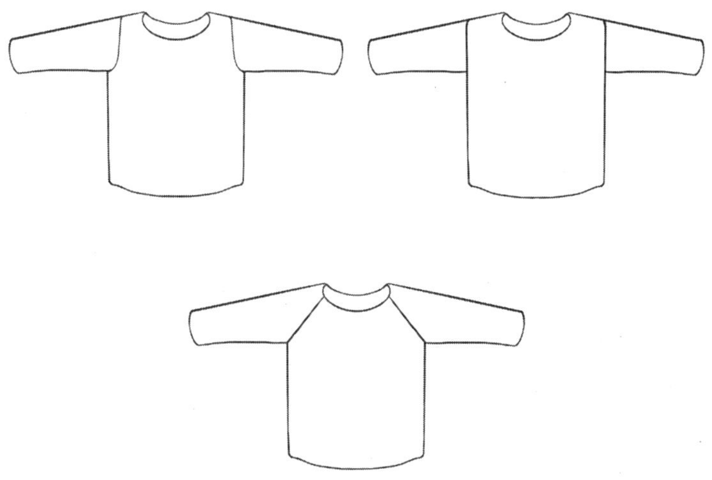

Top left: Sweater with set-in sleeves. Top right: Sweater with drop shoulders. Bottom: Raglan.

One-piece raglans and circular yoke garments don't have separate sleeve caps; instead, the upper portion of the sleeve is incorporated into the yoke structure. In this case you look at the yoke depth.

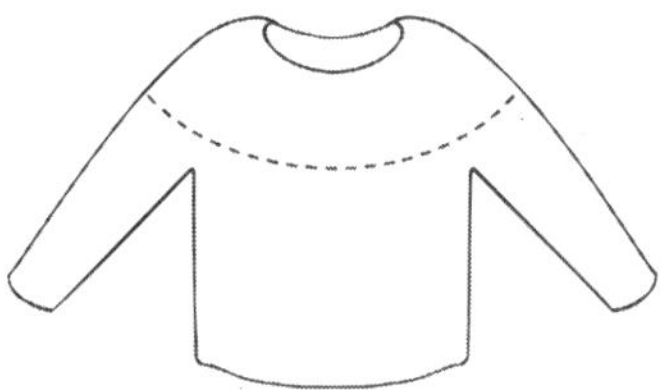

Sweater with a circular yoke.

Sleeve length alterations are always made below the underarm, below any yoke or cap. (As noted earlier, altering sleeve caps and yokes is complicated, and, with the exception of raglans, is beyond the scope of this book. See this chapter, Adjusting a Seamless Raglan Garment for a Different Row/Round Gauge, on page 147 for information about adjusting raglan depth. To make sure that the garment you've chosen fits you well in that area, see chapter Garment Math 1: Size, Fit, and Ease.)

Step 1: Determine the Garment's Centre-Back-Neck-to-Underarm Measurement

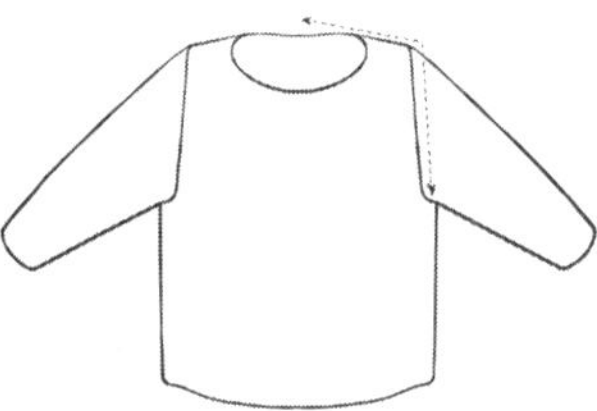

To determine the proper sleeve length, you need the measurement of the garment from the centre back neck to where the garment underarm hits.

For a set-in sleeve garment, or a raglan worked in pieces, this is:

`Half the width of the back neck + the width of one shoulder + the sleeve cap depth.`

For a drop shoulder garment, this is:

`Half the width of the back neck + the width of one shoulder.`

For a raglan worked in pieces, this is:

`Half the width of the back neck + the sleeve cap depth.`

For a seamless raglan or circular yoke, this is:

`Half the width of the back neck + the yoke depth.`

Step 2: Determine Desired Sleeve Length

This is not a measurement you can take on yourself—you'll need help!

Look at the garment's centre-back-neck-to-shoulder measurement, and compare that to your own body: Get your helper to hold the tape measure at the centre of the back of your neck, and measure across your shoulder and down along your arm, to the length you calculated above. This is where the sleeve starts. From that point, measure down to where you want the sleeve hem to hit.

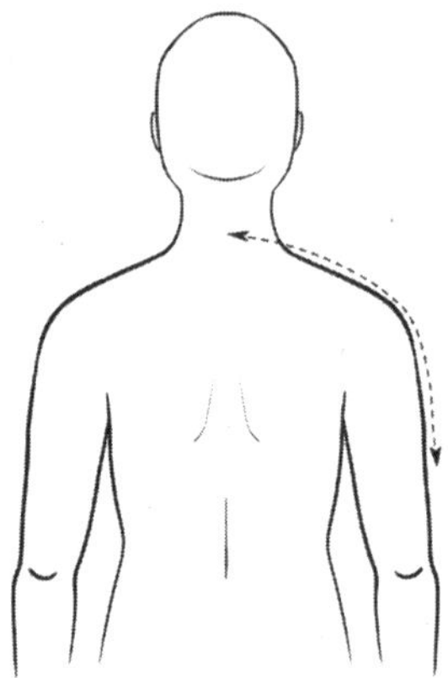

How to measure for sleeve length.

Adjusting for Longer or Shorter Arms

Level of Difficulty: ◆◆

If you're looking to add or remove length from a sleeve to adjust for a different arm length (or a different row gauge), you will keep the stitch counts at top and bottom, and redistribute the shaping along the sleeve.

A Shortcut for a Small Adjustment

If the difference between the pattern length and your desired length is small, for example, less than two inches/4–5 cm or so, then you may well be able to handle it without significant reworking. (Any longer than that, and this solution would throw off the position of the shaping.)

Consult your pattern. There's usually some length worked even (without increasing or decreasing) before the shaping begins and after the final shaping is worked. In a top-down sweater, you usually work a few rounds at the full stitch count before starting to decrease, and a few rounds after the last decrease is worked—before you start the cuff. In a bottom-up sweater, you work even for a distance between the cuff and the first increase, and then again for a short distance after the last increase. If you need to add length, do it in these two sections—half at the top and half at the bottom. You may also be able to remove a little length within these sections, but that requires a bit of careful pattern reading to determine how much space you have to work with.

Find these numbers in the pattern:

- Stitch count just below underarms (before armhole shaping if you're working bottom up, after armhole increases if you're working top down)
- Stitch count in main fabric just above edging
- Depth of cuff edging (this can be customized, too)

Make a note of:

- Your row/round gauge

Measure:

- The full length you want for the sleeve, from underarm to lower edge (see Steps 1 and 2)

Determine:

- The working sleeve length
  - `Working sleeve length = full sleeve length - the depth of the cuff.`

Calculate:

- The distribution of the shaping along working length between the underarm and the cuff (see Garment Math: The Calculations – Distributing Shaping on page 162)

Working the adjusted sleeve:

- For a bottom-up garment
    1. Cast on and work cuff as written in the pattern.
    2. Work increases as calculated, to the underarm.
    3. Resume working from the pattern, beginning with any sleeve cap shaping.

- For a top-down garment

1. Starting below the underarm/sleeve separation, work shaping as calculated, to desired length to cuff.
2. Work the cuff and bind off as written.

Changing the Sleeve Style

Level of Difficulty: ◆◆◆

In this case, you are changing where the sleeve cuff hits on your arm. For this, you will also need to adjust the cuff.

Find these numbers in the pattern:

- Stitch count just below underarms (before armhole shaping if you're working bottom up, after armhole increases if you're working top down)
- Stitch counts at existing cuff (in main fabric just above the edging and in the edging pattern)

- Depth of cuff edging (this can be customized, too)

Make a note of:

- Your stitch gauge (the assumption is that your working stitch gauge matches the gauge the pattern is calculated for. See this chapter, An Important Note About Gauge on page 110)
- Your row/round gauge

Measure:

- The length of your desired sleeve, from underarm to lower edge (see Steps 1 and 2)
- The circumference of your arm where you want the lower edge of the sleeve to hit

Determine:

- The working sleeve length
    - Working sleeve length = full sleeve length - the depth of the cuff.
- Desired circumferences at lower edge of sleeve
    - Lower edge circumference = your actual arm circumference at that point × sleeve ease factor.
    - (See on page 144 for notes on sleeve ease factor)

Calculate:

- Stitch counts for lower edge of sleeve (use Garment Math: The Calculations – Method B: Stitch Counts for Hems and Lower Edges on page 158)

  - Edging stitch count
  - Stitch count in main fabric (above the edging)
  - Edging/Main Fabric Transition
- Distribute shaping along working length between the underarm and the cuff (see Garment Math: The Calculations – Distributing Shaping on page 162)

Working the adjusted sleeve:

- For a bottom-up garment
  1. Cast on calculated stitch count for the edging, and work the edging stitch pattern as given.
  2. Work an edging/main fabric transition if required.
  3. Work increases as calculated, to the underarm.
  4. Resume working from the pattern, beginning with any sleeve cap shaping.

- For a top-down garment
  1. Starting below the underarm/sleeve separation, work shaping as calculated, to desired length to cuff.
  2. Work an edging/main fabric transition if required.
  3. Work edging stitch pattern on your calculated stitch count, and bind off.

Determining the Circumference of Your Sleeve at the Lower Edge: Sleeve Ease Factor

There should always be positive ease around the lower sleeve and cuff—more than you might expect. (A too-tight sleeve cuff can be very uncomfortable, and doesn't move when you bend your arm.) Generally, I keep the ease for the sleeve cuff in line with the original pattern.

Take the circumference of your own arm around where the original sleeve cuff hits, and look at the circumference of the original sleeve for your size, just above the ribbing/edging. (If you're not sure what that is, divide the stitch count just above the cuff edging by the gauge for the main sleeve fabric.)

```
Sleeve ease factor = original sleeve
circumference ÷ your arm circumference
at that point.
```

For example, if the original sleeve is 9 inches/23cm around, and your wrist is 7 inches/18.5 cm the sleeve ease factor is

```
9 inches ÷ 7 inches = 1.3.
```

Or, if you're working in metric:

```
23 cm ÷ 18.5 cm = 1.3.
```

Take your arm measurement at the point you want the sleeve to hit, and multiply that by the sleeve ease factor.

If your arm circumference where you want the sleeve to hit measures 8.5 inches/21.5 cm, calculate the lower sleeve circumference by multiplying that measurement by 1.3.

```
Lower sleeve circumference = 8.5 inches
× 1.3 = 11 inches.
```

Or, if you're working in metric:

```
Lower sleeve circumference = 21.5 cm ×
1.3 = 28 cm.
```

ADJUSTING FOR A DIFFERENT ROW/ROUND GAUGE

Note: See the chapter Gauge Math 201: Converting for a Different Gauge for advice on when this adjustment applies, and when it doesn't.

General Row/Round Gauge Adjustments

Level of Difficulty: ◆◆

A row gauge adjustment is exactly the same as a length adjustment, you use the same information and make the same calculations.

When it's just a case of working on the same stitch count to a specific length, no calculations are required, but remember that yarn usage will change. Row gauge adjustments come into play when there's shaping being worked.

Find these numbers in the pattern:

- Stitch count at starting and ending points
    - If there's an edging, work with the main fabric stitch counts only
- The lengths you are to match
    - E.g., the length of waist shaping for a garment, a mitten thumb gusset depth, hat crown decreases
- If the section has an edging, e.g., a garment body piece with a ribbed hem, or a sleeve with a cuff
    - Depth of edging (this can be customized, too)

Make a note of:

- Your row/round gauge

Determine:

- The working length, if required
    - `Working length = total length of piece - depth of the edging.`

Calculate:

- The row/round count at the new gauge
    - If you're working in inches
        - Number of rows/rounds = length × rows/rounds per inch.
    - If you're working in metric
        - Number of rows/rounds = length × rows/rounds per cm.
- The distribution of the shaping from starting point to ending point, along working length
- (See Garment Math: The Calculations – Distributing Shaping on page 162)

Working the adjusted piece:

1. Work edging as required, either at top or bottom.
2. Distribute shaping as calculated, along working length.

Adjusting a Seamless Raglan Garment for a Different Row/Round Gauge

Level of Difficulty: ◆◆◆

There are two distinct sections to be adjusted:

1. The lower body and sleeves—these can be handled with the method outlined above.

2. The yoke—uses the same basic strategy, but there are some potential complexities.

A standard raglan uses one shaping round, with two "shapings"—either increases or decreases—worked at each seam point where the upper sleeve meets the body. This is the most straightforward to alter, as it is a single calculation: distributing the shaping along the adjusted row count, using the method outlined above.

Some raglan garments use a "compound" shaping, meaning that the rate of shaping is different for the sleeve and the body. You can identify a garment constructed like this by examining the pattern. If it's worked in the round, you'll see instructions for shaping rounds that work fewer than eight increases; if worked flat in pieces, the shaping instructions will be different for the body pieces compared to the sleeve pieces.

If this is the case, then you will need to calculate the shaping separately for the two sections.

In addition, for either a standard or compound raglan, there's often neckline shaping worked, and that will need to be adjusted, too. For example, a top-down raglan worked in one piece may start in rows, with increases worked at the beginning and end of the rows for the centre front neck. These will also need to be adjusted.

Adjusting a Seamless Circular Yoke Garment for a Different Row/Round Gauge

Level of Difficulty: ◆◆

There are two distinct sections to be adjusted:

1. The lower body and sleeves (use the method outlined in the previous section for adjusting these)

2. The yoke

To adjust the yoke in this case, you'll need to confirm the shaping strategy used in the pattern. Most circular yokes are constructed by working a small number of shaping rounds, often 3–6, placed at specific distances along the depth of the yoke. If this is the case, then the adjustment is remarkably straightforward. Use the pattern round/row gauge to work out the distance between the shaping rounds/rows, and then use the new round/row gauge to calculate the round count.

> **Don't Adjust the Distances!**
> There are rules for the placement of these shaping rounds. See Amy Herzog's *Ultimate Sweater Book* for more information.

GOING FURTHER

You can use similar methods and calculations for some other types of key adjustments: neckline shape and depth, and a clever strategy for creating a better fit around a larger bust.

Neckline Depth, Crew Neck and V-neck Changes

Level of Difficulty: ◆◆

For collar planning purposes, note that crewneck shaping can be used as the basis for a turtleneck or cowl-style collar; a V-neck forms the basis of a shawl collar for a cardigan. Creating or adjusting a crewneck or a V-neck on a garment is reasonably straightforward.

Neckline Adjustment Guidelines

- Leave the back neck width and shoulder widths/stitch counts alone; do not adjust those.

- For a crew neck, use the pattern number for the stitch count for the central, flat portion of the neckline.
- For a pullover, neckline depth + neckline width (taking the edging into account) must be at least half of your head circumference, otherwise you won't be able to get it over your head.
- If you adjust neckline shape or depth, the number of stitches picked up for edgings will also need to be adjusted. For this, use the same ratios for picking up stitches that the pattern uses. See Quick Reference: Ratios for Picking Up Stitches on page 179.

V-necks:

- A V-neck is typically worked so that the lower edge is aligned with the base of the armhole.
- Lowering the start of the neck opening is straightforward.
- Raising the start of the neck opening introduces two risks:
    - A too-high neck means a too-small opening that can be harder to get over your head.
    - For a body that has breasts, a higher neck opening can create a potentially unflattering optical illusion in which the breasts to seem lower. We are so used to the relative proportions of the neckline and armholes on a V-neck that when these proportions are "off," (e.g., when the neckline is raised), it can appear to distort the wearer's body shape. Although this is true for all necklines, it's worse for a V-neck.
- Calculate the number of stitches to be increased/decreased for the neckline:

    - `Number of stitches to be increased/decreased on each side for the neckline = [total number of stitches in upper front after armhole shaping – the total number of stitches in both shoulders] ÷ 2`
- Working bottom up, you're working decreases. Working top-down, you're working increases.
- Adjusting the depth of a V-neck is just a case of distributing the shaping along a different number of rows.

Crew necks:

- Working bottom up, any neckline shaping should be complete about 3–5 cm/1.5–2 inches before the top. If the garment has shoulder shaping, the neckline shaping should be complete before the shoulder shaping starts.
- If working top down, neckline increases should start about 3–5 cm/1.5–2 inches from the cast on.
- Calculate the number of stitches to be increased/decreased for the neckline:
    - `Number of stitches to be increased/decreased on each side for the neckline = [total number of stitches in upper front after armhole shaping – the total number of stitches in both shoulders] ÷ 2`
- Working bottom up, you're working decreases. Working top-down you're working increases.
- The shaping is worked in three stages.
    - If working bottom up, bind off the centre third of the neckline stitches in one row. Divide the

remaining two thirds of the stitches in half, to determine how many should be decreased each side. Of those, decrease half of them every other row, and the other half every fourth row, or so, as row gauge permits. (If you don't have enough rows to follow that pattern, put more decreases in the second stage, and fewer in the third.)

  - If working top-down, divide up the neckline stitches. One third should be cast on when you reach the full neckline depth. Divide the remaining two thirds of the stitches in half, to determine how many should be increased each side. Distribute the increases across the rows in the neckline depth, aiming to increase about half of them approximately every fourth row in the first step, and increasing the other half every other row in the second step.

See Amy Herzog's *The Ultimate Sweater Book* (see Further Reading on page 180).

Different Size Front & Back

Level of Difficulty: ◆◆◆

This is a good solution for when

- The body you are fitting has a significantly larger full bust circumference than upper bust circumference. See the chapter Garment Math 1: Size, Fit, and Ease for more details on this.
- The chosen size of the garment fits well in the shoulders and upper body, but doesn't have sufficient ease to clear the fullest part of the bust, and the next size (or two) up has sufficient width to accommodate

the fullest part of the bust. (If you're jumping more than a couple of sizes, or there's a massive gap between the size for the back and the size for the front, there could be more challenges in getting the pieces to fit together. See the chapter Garment Math 1: Size, Fit, and Ease.)

It's relatively straightforward for a garment worked bottom up, either in the round or in pieces. For a garment worked top-down in the round, it's a more complex adjustment. See Amy Herzog's *The Ultimate Sweater Book* (see Further Reading on page 180).

At a high level, here's how it works:

For a bottom-up garment worked in pieces

- Work the back and sleeves for the chosen size, as written.
- Work a hybrid for the front of the garment, using the stitch counts and widths of the larger size, and the lengths for the original size.
  - If the garment has lower body/waist shaping, follow the shaping pattern from the smaller size.
- Work armhole shaping as written for the smaller size; incorporate additional decreases into the neckline shaping so that you hit the shoulder stitch count for the smaller size.

For a bottom-up garment worked in the round

- Adjust the lower body stitch count: ½ of the smaller size for the back + ½ of the larger size for the front.
- Work any lower body/waist shaping as written for the smaller size

- Work armhole shaping as written for the smaller size, but ensure your armhole division is offset, relative to the adjusted stitch count. That is, when dividing for the front and back, place markers at the sides to separate the two sections relative to the adjusted stitch counts. Then work any bind offs and decreases for the smaller size, centred around those markers.
- Work decreases in the upper body/neckline to hit the shoulder stitch count for the smaller size.

For a top-down garment worked in the round

- Adjust the lower body stitch count: ½ of the smaller size for the back + ½ of the larger size for the front.
- Adjust the division of the cast on stitches, to allocate more stitches to the front section(s), than the back.
    - Front offset = adjusted stitch count for the front - original stitch count for the front.
    - Increase the stitches allocated to the front by the offset, and decrease the stitches allocated to the back by the same number.
    - If the piece starts flat, whether it's a cardigan or there are neckline increases to be worked, divide the offset between the two front sections.

CHAPTER 9
GARMENT MATH: THE CALCULATIONS

There are only two types of calculations: determining stitch counts and distributing shaping.

Determining stitch counts:

```
Desired size of the piece you want to make × the number of stitches per inch (or cm for metric) = stitch count.
```

Distributing shaping:

```
Total number of rows/rounds ÷ the number or increases or decrease rows/rounds you have to do = the spacing of the shaping rows/rounds.
```

I've broken the calculations out this way because any type of adjustment relies on these two methods—and many of them only need one. Really! Once you've got the hang of a couple of concepts and a couple of methods, you can do anything.

Distributing Shaping

Distributing shaping works in exactly the same way as distributing increases, decreases or buttonholes in a row. Once you've mastered that, you are well prepared for this.

Each specific alteration, as detailed in the previous chapter, outlines which numbers and methods are used.

STITCH COUNTS

The Fundamental Rules

- The actual measurement of a piece for a garment = body measurement + ease. See the chapter Garment Math 1: Size, Fit, and Ease.
- If the body of the garment or sleeve is worked plain—that is, in garter, stockinette stitch or reverse stockinette stitch—determine if your calculated stitch counts need to be even or odd.
    - Look at the stitch count just under the armhole shaping. If that's even (i.e., a multiple of two), round all your calculated stitch counts to be even. If the under-armhole stitch count is odd, round all your calculated stitch counts to be odd.
- If your garment body is worked in one piece, either a pullover in the round or a cardigan worked flat (or in the round for steeking), then use the full garment circumference measurement to calculate stitch counts.
- If you are making a pullover body in two pieces to be sewn up, divide the garment body measurement in half to calculate the width of the back and front pieces, and use that to calculate stitch counts.
- If you are making a cardigan body in three pieces to be sewn up, divide the garment body measurement

in half to calculate the width of the back piece, divide that in half to calculate the widths of the two front pieces, and then use those to calculate stitch counts.

- Sleeves are always worked in one piece; use the full sleeve circumference to calculate stitch counts.
- If you're adjusting the lower edge of a garment body or a sleeve, you might need two stitch counts, one for the edging pattern, and one for the main fabric. In this case, there will also need to be a row/round that adjusts the stitch count, the edging/main fabric transition.

Method A: Stitch Counts for the Middle of a Piece

Use this method for sections of the garment that aren't adjacent to an edging, for example, at the waist of a sweater.

Numbers needed:

- The measurement of the piece
- The stitch gauge in stitches per inch or cm

Calculate stitch count:

- Working in inches
  - `Stitch count = Measurement of piece × stitches per inch.`
- Working in metric
  - `Stitch count = Measurement of piece × stitches per cm.`

Adjust this to be a whole number, and even or odd as required. (See above.) If there's a pattern stitch, for example, ribbing, confirm that the repeat fits into your calculated stitch count.

See Garment Math 2: Alterations – Changing Edgings on page 114.

Method B: Stitch Counts for Hems and Lower Edges

Use this method when you have both an edging pattern stitch and main fabric, for example, if a sleeve cuff has ribbing and the body of the sleeve is worked in stockinette stitch.

In this case, you need to calculate the stitch count for the main fabric required at that point, the stitch count for the adjacent section of edging (worked in the appropriate pattern stitch), and any required stitch count transition.

Numbers needed:

- The measurement of the piece
- The stitch gauge in stitches per inch or cm
- Stitch count in edging pattern of the original piece at or near the position you're calculating for
- Stitch count in main fabric of original piece at or near the position you're calculating for

<u>If Edging and Main Fabrics Are Worked on the Same Stitch Count</u>

Use the gauge for your main fabric.

Step 1: Calculate stitch count for main fabric.

- Working in inches:
  - `Measurement of piece × stitches per inch.`
- Working in metric:
  - `Measurement of piece × stitches per cm.`

Step 2: Confirm edging pattern stitch fit.

- If working in the round, you need an even multiple of the pattern repeat, e.g., a multiple of 4 for (k2, p2) ribbing.
- If working flat, and the piece is going to be seamed or have stitches picked up and knit along both sides, remember that the first and last stitch of the row will disappear into the seam. Make sure your stitch count is an even multiple of your pattern repeat, plus 2. To make it easy to seam, knit the first and last stitch of the row, on all rows, and work the pattern stitch between these two edging stitches.

For more on this, see Garment Math 2: Alterations – Changing Edgings on page 114.

Adjust the edging stitch count as required.

Step 3: Determine if a stitch count transition is necessary.

- If edging stitch count = main fabric stitch count, no transition is needed.
- If edging stitch count ≠ main fabric stitch count, see Step 5 in the next example.

If Edging and Main Fabrics Are Worked on Different Stitch Counts

Step 1: Calculate stitch count for main fabric.

- If working in inches:
    - `Measurement of piece × stitches per inch.`

- If working in metric:
    - `Measurement of piece × stitches per cm.`

Step 2: Calculate edging to main fabric ratio.

- Edging to main fabric ratio = original stitch count for edging ÷ original stitch count in main fabric.

Step 3:

- Edging stitch count = main fabric stitch count × edging to main ratio.

Step 4: Confirm edging pattern stitch fit.

- If working in the round, you need an even multiple of the pattern repeat, e.g., a multiple of 4 for (k2, p2) ribbing.
- If working flat, and the piece is going to be seamed or have stitches picked up and knit along both sides, remember that the first and last stitch of the row will disappear into the seam. Make sure your stitch count is an even multiple of your pattern repeat, plus 2. To make it easy to seam, knit the first and last stitch of the row, on all rows, and work the pattern stitch between these two edging stitches. (For more on this, see Garment Math 2: Alterations – Changing Edgings on page 114.)
- Adjust the edging stitch count as required.

Step 5: Calculate the edging/main fabric transition.

If adjusted edging stitch count = main fabric stitch count, no transition is needed.

Otherwise, determine if you are increasing or decreasing:

- Which fabric is worked first? Main or edging?
- Which fabric has the larger stitch count; which has the smaller stitch count?

If you're transitioning from a smaller stitch count to a larger, then you'll be working increases; if you're transitioning from a larger stitch count, then you'll be working decreases.

If increasing:

- `Transition count = larger stitch count - smaller stitch count.`
- `Increase spacing = smaller stitch count ÷ transition count.`
    - If the result is a whole number (i.e., no decimal places), then that sets the stitches in your increase repeat.
    - If there's a remainder, then distribute the extra stitches between your increase repeats.
    - If working in the round, work the increase at the beginning or end of your increase repeats.
    - If working flat, work the increase in the middle of the increase repeats.

For details on how to space these out neatly, refer to the chapter Pattern Reading Math 2: Evenly Across, and this chapter Evenly Across: Distributing Increases or Decreases in a Set of Stitches on page 171.

If decreasing:

- `Transition count = Larger stitch count - smaller stitch count.`
- `Decrease spacing = Larger stitch count ÷ Transition count.`
    - If the result is a whole number (i.e., no decimal places), then that sets the stitches in your decrease repeat.
    - If there's a remainder, then distribute the extra stitches between your decrease repeats.
    - If working in the round, work the decrease at the beginning or end of your decrease repeats.
    - If working flat, work the decrease in the middle of the decrease repeats.

For details on how to space these out neatly, refer to the chapter Pattern Reading Math 2: Evenly Across, and this chapter Evenly Across: Distributing Increases or Decreases in a Set of Stitches on page 171.

DISTRIBUTING SHAPING

This method is also used in the examples in the chapter Gauge Math 201: Converting for a Different Gauge. See that chapter for more examples of how it works, and some specific examples of how you might apply it.

The Guidelines

- When distributing shaping along a length, work about an inch/2–3 cm at maximum/minimum stitch counts, by making sure there are a few plain rows/rounds near the bottom and top.

- When shaping a sleeve, increases and decreases are worked two at a time.
    - If working flat, they are placed near the beginning and end of the rows, near the underarm seam.
    - If working in the round, they are placed a couple of stitches apart, centred under the arm. The start of the round is usually in this place, and so the shaping falls near the start and end of the round.
- When shaping the back and front of a pullover worked flat and sewn up, increases and decreases are worked two at a time.
    - They are usually placed near the beginning and end of the rows.
- When shaping the fronts of a cardigan worked flat and sewn up, increases and decreases are worked one at a time.
    - They are usually placed closed to the side seam edge, opposite to the opening edge.
- When shaping the body of a pullover worked in the round, or a cardigan worked in one piece, increases and decreases are worked four at a time.
    - They're usually placed two per side centred under the arms, a couple of stitches apart.

When working in rows:

- When calculating the number of rows in a length, it's much easier if you always round off the numbers so you're working with an even number of rows.
- When calculating row repeats, make sure there's an even number in each repeat. That is, if you're doing an increase or a decrease row, you need an odd

number of rows worked after. This keeps the increase and decrease rows always on the RS of your work.

When working in the round:

- The number of rounds in your round repeats don't matter—it can be even or odd.

The Shaping Rows/Rounds: What Do You Actually Knit?

If you're working with a pattern that already has increases or decreases rows or rounds written out, , the simplest answer is to use the specific increase or decrease rows/rounds from the pattern.

See Pattern Reading Math – Increase and Decrease Rows: "Increase at Each End," "Decrease at Each End," "Increase at Start," "Increase at End" on page 47 for examples of rows/rounds when you're increasing or decreasing two at a time.

For one increase or decrease at a time, use the one on the end of the row you need, working even at the other end.

If working four increases/decreases at a time, for example on a pullover body in the round, place markers centred under the arm and work one either side of the markers.

- Slightly less prominent: `(work to 3 sts before marker ssk, k1, marker, k1, k2tog).`
- Slightly more prominent: `(work to 3 sts before marker k2tog, k1, marker, k1, k2tog).`
- If your start of round marker is under one of the arms, then

you'll begin with the first post-marker decrease, and end with a pre-marker decrease.

And of course, you can always change both the increases and decreases used, and their position, if you wish.

Distribute Shaping

Numbers needed:

- The starting stitch count and the ending stitch count; one will be larger than the other
- The number of increases or decreases worked at a time: 1, 2, or 4
- The distance you are working over
    - A number of rows/rounds, OR
    - The length and the row/round gauge

Important Note: When Distributing Shaping, Stitch Counts Might Change Slightly

If you're working a piece with single increases or decreases (for example, a cardigan front), no adjustments will be needed.

But for most garment pieces, increases and decreases are worked in multiples: two or four at a time. For example, when you are working a sleeve, you always increase or decrease two stitches at a time.

Therefore, if the starting stitch count is an odd number, the ending stitch count will need to be odd, too. As noted in The Fundamental Rules at the very start of the section, when calculating stitch counts, you need to check whether your "anchor" stitch count—that is, the one you're working to from the pattern (usually the underarm number)—is even or odd, and match that.

That resolves the issue for sleeves and garment fronts and backs that are worked flat. But if you are calculating shaping for a garment worked in the round that has four increases or decreases worked at a time, then you might need to adjust stitch counts to make sure you can "get there from here." That is, if the garment has 200 stitches under the arm, and I calculate that I need 174 stitches at the waist, I'm in trouble.

```
200 - 174 = 26.
26 ÷ 4 = 6.5.
```

This means that you can't decrease from 200 to 176, 4 stitches at time. Always keep the "anchor" garment stitch count and tweak your own calculated numbers. In this case, I should either use 172 or 176 for my waist stitch count.

Step 1: Calculate the number of shaping rows/rounds to work, and adjust stitch counts if required.

- `Number of shaping rows/rounds = (Larger stitch count - smaller stitch count) ÷ number of stitches increased/decreased at a time.`

The result of this division should be a whole number; if it's not, you'll need to adjust one of the stitch counts. For example, if you're decreasing by 2 stitches at time, both numbers will need to be either even or odd.

Step 2: Calculate the number of rows/rounds in the distance, if required.

- If working in inches:
    - `Total rows/rounds = Length × rows/rounds per inch.`
- If working in metric:
    - `Total rows/rounds = Length × rows/rounds per cm.`

Shaping Repeat

I'm using the term "shaping repeat" to mean the row-repeat or round-repeat that sets the spacing, that is, if you're increasing every 4 rows, that's a 4-row shaping repeat.

Step 3: Calculate the shaping repeat—working in the round.

Note: If you're working in rows, see Step 3 for working in rows, below.

- `Shaping repeat = Total rounds ÷ Number of shaping rounds.`
    - If the result is a whole number, then that sets the number of rounds in your shaping repeat.
    - If there's a remainder, then distribute the extra rounds between your repeats.
    - There isn't a single correct answer here, as long as your shaping rounds are roughly evenly distributed and there's about an inch/2–3 cm of even (non-shaping) rounds at the start and the end, you're good!

Example

For example, if you have 100 rounds total, and you have to work 5 decrease rounds:

`100 ÷ 5 = 20.`

This means you have 5 sets of 20 rounds.

If you place the shaping round in the middle of the 20, you'll get a short even distance before the first and after the last, for example,

`(9 even rounds, 1 shaping round, 10 even rounds) 5 times.`

Example

For example, if you have 60 rounds total, and you have to work 8 decrease rounds:

`60 ÷ 8 = 7.5.`

This means you have 8 sets of 7 rounds, and a remainder of 4 rounds.

`60 = 8 × 7 + 4.`

Try a few versions to see which works well for you. Consider placing the shaping around at the end of the 7-round repeat, and working the 4 extra at the end, as follows:

`(6 even rounds, 1 shaping round) 8 times, 4 even rounds.`

Step 3: Calculate the shaping repeat—working in rows.

Use this version of Step 3 if you're working rows.

- `Shaping repeat = Total rows ÷ Number of shaping rows`

- If the result is a whole, even number, then that sets the number of rows in your shaping repeat.
- If the result is an odd number, or there's a remainder, round down so that the number of rows in your shaping repeat is even, and then distribute the extra rows between your repeats.
- There isn't a single correct answer here, as long as your shaping rows are roughly evenly distributed and there's about an inch/2-3 cm of even (non-shaping) rows at the start and the end, you're good!

Example

For example, if you have 100 rows total, and you have to work 5 decrease rows:

`100 ÷ 5 = 20.`

This means you have 5 sets of 20 rows.

If you place the shaping rows in the middle of the 20, you'll get a short even distance before the first and after the last, for example,

`(10 even rows, 1 shaping rows, 9 even rows) 5 times.`

In this case, the shaping row is on the 11th row, so that it falls on a RS row.

Note: This example assumes that you're starting with a RS row. Either way, make sure that the total number of rows in the repeat is even, that is, divides by two, and that you work your shaping row on a RS row.

Example

For example, if you have 60 rows total, and you have to work 8 decrease rows:

`60 ÷ 8 = 7.5.`

This suggests you have 8 sets of 7 rows, and a remainder of 4.

`60 = 8 × 7 + 4.`

This doesn't work, because having an odd number of rows in a row-repeat would force you to work your shaping on both RS and WS rows. You need an even number of rows in your row-repeat.

Round down, so that your base row-repeat has 6 rows.

This covers 48 rows: a 6-row-repeat 8 times; but you then have 12 additional rows to account for. This gives you the following:

`(Shaping row, 5 even rows) 8 times, 12 even rows.`

Stick 6 of them at the start, so you've got some even distance at both start and end.

`6 even rows, (shaping row, 5 even rows) 8 times, 6 even rows.`

Split those final 6 rows up, two at a time, and add them into some of the repeats, giving you an 8-row-repeat three times, and a 6-row-repeat five times.

`6 even rows, (shaping row, 5 even rows) 5 times, (shaping row, 7 even rows) 3 times.`

Evenly Across: Distributing Increases or Decreases in a Set of Stitches

In the chapter Pattern Reading Math 2: Evenly Across, we learned how to handle an instruction that asks you to increase or decrease evenly across a set of stitches, in one row or round.

This type of calculation is needed for transition rows and rounds—when you're working the plain section of a garment in one pattern stitch, and an adjacent edging in another, but they require different stitch counts.

If you work through some examples below, you will notice something: You use exactly the same method that we learned in the section about distributing shaping.

And it works for both stitches and rows!

For example, if you need to work 3 decreases rows in 18 rows, you would proceed as follows:

```
18 rows total ÷ 3 increase rows = 6.
```

The answer here, 6, gives you the row-repeat. This means that you've got 3 sets of 6 rows, adding up to 18. And in each of those sets of 6 rows you need to work an increase row—that is, work 5 of them even and one of them as an increase row.

To space them evenly, I'd choose to place the increase row in the middle of the row-repeat, for example,

```
(2 rows even, increase row, 3 rows even) 3 times.
```

But what if this was stitches, and you needed to increase 3 times in 8 stitches? The calculations are the same.

```
18 stitches ÷ 3 increases = 6.
```

The answer here, 6, gives you the repeat. This means that you've got 3 sets of 6 stitches, adding up to 18. An in each of those sets of 6 stitches, you need to work an increase.

To space them evenly, place the increase in the middle of the repeat, for example,

```
(k3, Make-1, k3) 3 times.
```

There is a bit of a difference here compared to how it works when you're dealing with rows or rounds. In that calculation, working increases or decreases "uses up" a row or round. But for increasing within a row, for the make 1 family, the increase sits in the gap between stitches.

If we were using a kfb increase, however, the result would be exactly the same for stitches and rows.

Instead of

```
(2 rows even, increase row, 3 rows even) 3 times
```

you would have

```
(k2, kfb, k3) 3 times.
```

When working an "evenly across" example with decreases, you need to account for the decrease itself in each group of stitches. The usual decreases, k2tog and ssk/skp, are worked over two stitches, so you need to allocate two in the group, making the repeat

```
(k2, k2tog, k2) 3 times.
```

To be explicit: all of the examples of "evenly across" instructions I've used so far are a relevant to a row of stitches for knitting worked flat, because when working flat you use the same "stick it in the middle" strategy that you use for distributing shaping rows/rounds in a set of rows/rounds.

But if you're working "evenly across" a set of stitches joined in the round, you can place the increase or decrease at the start or end of the group of stitches.

And of course, if the division doesn't work out evenly—if you've got a remainder to deal with—you can choose to put that at the start or end, or distribute through the groups of stitches/rows as you prefer.

One method, so many applications!

APPENDICES

GLOSSARY

This isn't a complete glossary of knitting terms, just for those used in this book.

cm: centimetre(s)

k2tog: Knit 2 stitches together; 1 stitch decreased.

kfb: Knit into the front and back of the stitch. 1 stitch increased.

LlI: Use tip of left needle to lift left leg of stitch 2 below the last worked on right needle, and knit into it. 1 stitch increased.

m: metre(s)

m1 or make-1: "make 1." Without further information or definition, the knitter can choose their preferred method of m1r or m1l; the backwards loop increase also works here.

m1r: Use the tip of the left needle to lift the strand that runs between the last stitch worked and the next stitch, from back to front; knit this strand through the front. 1 stitch increased.

m1l: Use the tip of the left needle to lift the strand that runs between the last stitch worked and the next stitch, from front to back; knit this strand through the back. 1 stitch increased.

pfb: Purl into the front and back of the stitch. 1 stitch increased.

RLI: Use tip of right needle to lift right leg of stitch below the first on left needle, place it on the left needle with right leg to the front, and knit into it. 1 stitch increased.

ssk: Slip the next 2 stitches, individually, knitwise; return them to the left needle without twisting, and knit them together through the back loop. 1 stitch decreased.

yd/yds: yard(s)

yo, yarnover: Bring the yarn to the front between the needle tips, and when working the next stitch let it drape over the right needle to make a new stitch. 1 stitch increased.

QUICK REFERENCE: NEEDLE SIZES

Metric size – US size

1.5 mm – US #000

1.75 mm – US #00

2 mm – US #0

2.25 mm – US #1

2.5 mm – No standard equivalent: some patterns list as #1.5

2.75 mm – US #2

3 mm – No standard equivalent: some patterns list as #2.5

3.25 mm – US #3

3.5 mm – US #4

3.75 mm – US #5

4 mm – US #6

4.5 mm – US #7

5 mm – US #8

5.5 mm – US #9

6 mm – US #10

6.5mm – US #10.5

7mm – No standard equivalent: some patterns list as #10¾

7.5mm – No standard equivalent

8mm – US #11

9mm – US #13

10mm – US #15

12mm – US #17—sometimes*

12.75mm – US #17—sometimes*

15mm – US #19

19mm – US #35

20mm – US #36

25mm – US #50

* *Note*: this US size is applied to two metric sizes; read the package carefully to know which you're getting. Although also note that when working with needles that large, the .75mm difference between the two is often inconsequential.

QUICK REFERENCE: RATIOS FOR PICKING UP STITCHES

<table>
<tr><th>Base Fabric</th><th>Edge of Pick-up</th><th>Fabric to be worked on picked-up stitches</th><th>Ratio</th></tr>
<tr><td>Any</td><td>Cast on or bind off</td><td>Any.
Note: if you will be working a different stitch pattern on the picked-up stitches, you may need to adjust the stitch count after pickup to compensate for a different gauge.</td><td>Pick-up and knit 1 stitch for every stitch.</td></tr>
<tr><td rowspan="3">Stockinette stitch, ribbing, other knit/ purl fabrics.</td><td rowspan="3">Side edge, diagonal edge</td><td>Stockinette stitch</td><td>Pick up and knit 3 stitches for every 4 rows.</td></tr>
<tr><td>Ribbing</td><td>Pick up and knit 3 stitches for every 4 rows.</td></tr>
<tr><td>Garter stitch</td><td>Pick up and knit 2 stitches for every 3 rows.</td></tr>
<tr><td>Garter stitch</td><td>Side edge</td><td>Any</td><td>Pick up and knit 1 stitches for every 2 rows.</td></tr>
</table>

FURTHER READING

Atherley, Kate (2015). *Custom Socks*. Interweave Press/Penguin Random House.

Atherley, Kate (2017). *Knit Mitts: Your Hand-y Guide to Knitting Mittens & Gloves*. Interweave Press/Krause Craft.

Atherley, Kate (2020). *Custom-Fit Hats*. Nine Ten Publications.

Herzog, Amy (2013). *Knit to Flatter.* STC Craft/A Melanie Falick Book.

Herzog, Amy (2018). *The Ultimate Sweater Book*. Abrams Books.

ACKNOWLEDGMENTS

Many thanks to Kim Werker, Michelle Woodvine and Jo Fromstein for their editing and moral support with this project, and for helping me get it over the finish line at last; and to Alison Cooley for drawings and schematics that illustrate the concepts in the book so perfectly.

Thanks to my preview readers, who provided valuable feedback on earlier versions of the manuscript: Alicia Aitchison, Meg Anderson Kilfoil, Cari Angold, Judy Brown, Casey Evans, Cheryl McLeod, Lynne Sosnowski, Sarah Thornton, Amy Vervoort, and Michelle Woodvine.

Much gratitude to Natalie Warner for her wise counsel and technical support.

And as always, all my love to Norman, without whom I'd still be working an uninteresting job at an uninspiring desk in an impersonal office tower.

ALSO BY KATE ATHERLEY FROM NINE TEN

A fun and different way to knit hats: from the top down.

This is not a standard pattern book — it's a complete recipe for making your own custom-fit hats, for any head, with any yarn. Just grab a skein and start knitting!

The book steps you through the whole process: from choosing yarn and determining size right through to finishing, with tutorials for all the key knitting techniques—casting on, working in the round, stretchy and decorative bind-offs, even weaving in the ends.

Whether you're a hat novice or an experienced knitter of headwear, this book has something for you!

ABOUT THE AUTHOR

KATE ATHERLEY has been teaching knitting professionally in Canada, the U.S. and the U.K. for 25 years, and she has written ten books about various aspects of knitting, including a series of four about customizing projects for perfect fit and style. Her focus in all her work is the empowerment of knitters, illuminating both the methods and mechanics of the craft. The combination of her university degree in mathematics, professional experience in software development and usability, and training in fashion design give her a unique perspective. She also works as a technical editor, helping other designers and authors bring their work into the world. She lives in Toronto with her husband and their rescue dog, Winnie.

www.kateatherley.com

Instagram/Threads: kateatherleyknits

BlueSky/Ravelry: kateatherley

MORE BOOKS FROM NINE TEN

Nine Ten publishes non-fiction books by Canadians on topics related to art, craft and creativity. Our mission is to serve readers who hunger for books that scratch beneath the surface of the topics they're passionate, nerdy, geeky and obsessive about. We print our books in Canada, on paper that has as much recycled content as we can afford (usually, that's 100%).

Find more fascinating books at shop.ninetenpublications.ca, at your local library, or at your favourite craft shop or bookstore.

@NineTenPub